THE AMERICAN POLITICAL NARRATIVE

FIRST EDITION

By Anthony Neal
Buffalo State College

Bassim Hamadeh, CEO and Publisher
Michael Simpson, Vice President of Acquisitions
Jamie Giganti, Senior Managing Editor
Jess Busch, Senior Graphic Designer
John Remington, Senior Field Acquisitions Editor
Monika Dziamka, Project Editor
Brian Fahey, Licensing Specialist
Claire Yee, Interior Designer

First published in the United States of America in 2016 by Cognella, Inc.

Printed in the United States of America

ISBN: 978-1-63487-408-3 (pbk) / 978-1-63487-409-0 (br)

www.cognella.com 800-200-3908

CONTENTS

1 THE AMERICAN REVOLUTIONARY CONTEXT

On July 23, 2013 Prince William and Duchess Kate became the proud parents of a baby boy. They announced that the child would be named George Alexander Louis. The birth of this child is significant because he will be in line of succession to the British throne. Not only is the child in line of succession to the throne, but the child could eventually be known as King George of England. The irony for the United States is that it was King George III against whom the original thirteen colonies rebelled, thus beginning the American Revolution and the road to independence. The colonists' indictments against the king were listed in Jefferson's Declaration of Independence, which was unanimously approved by the Second Continental Congress:

> *He has refused his assent to laws, the most wholesome and necessary for the public good.*
>
> *He has forbidden his governors to pass laws of immediate and pressing importance, unless suspended in their operation till his assent should be obtained; and when so suspended, he has utterly neglected to attend to them.*
>
> *He has refused to pass other laws for the accommodation of large districts of people, unless those people would*

relinquish the right of representation in the legislature, a right inestimable to them and formidable to tyrants only.

He has called together legislative bodies at places unusual, uncomfortable, and distant from the depository of their public records, for the sole purpose of fatiguing them into compliance with his measures.

He has dissolved representative houses repeatedly, for opposing with manly firmness his invasions on the rights of the people.

He has refused for a long time, after such dissolutions, to cause others to be elected; whereby the legislative powers, incapable of annihilation, have returned to the people at large for their exercise; the state remaining in the meantime exposed to all the dangers of invasion from without, and convulsions within.

He has endeavored to prevent the population of these states; for that purpose obstructing the laws for naturalization of foreigners; refusing to pass others to encourage their migration hither, and raising the conditions of new appropriations of lands.

He has obstructed the administration of justice, by refusing his assent to laws for establishing judiciary powers.

He has made judges dependent on his will alone, for the tenure of their offices, and the amount and payment of their salaries.

He has erected a multitude of new offices, and sent hither swarms of officers to harass our people, and eat out their substance.

He has kept among us, in times of peace, standing armies without the consent of our legislature.

He has affected to render the military independent of and superior to civil power.

He has combined with others to subject us to a jurisdiction foreign to our constitution, and unacknowledged by our laws; giving his assent to their acts of pretended legislation:

For quartering large bodies of armed troops among us:

For protecting them, by mock trial, from punishment for any murders which they should commit on the inhabitants of these states:

For cutting off our trade with all parts of the world:

For imposing taxes on us without our consent:

For depriving us in many cases, of the benefits of trial by jury:

For transporting us beyond seas to be tried for pretended offenses:

For abolishing the free system of English laws in a neighboring province, establishing therein an arbitrary government, and enlarging its boundaries so as to render it at once an example and fit instrument for introducing the same absolute rule in these colonies:

For taking away our charters, abolishing our most valuable laws, and altering fundamentally the forms of our governments:

For suspending our own legislatures, and declaring themselves invested with power to legislate for us in all cases whatsoever.

He has abdicated government here, by declaring us out of his protection and waging war against us.

> *He has plundered our seas, ravaged our coasts, burned our towns, and destroyed the lives of our people.*
>
> *He is at this time transporting large armies of foreign mercenaries to complete the works of death, desolation and tyranny, already begun with circumstances of cruelty and perfidy scarcely paralleled in the most barbarous ages, and totally unworthy the head of a civilized nation.*
>
> *He has constrained our fellow citizens taken captive on the high seas to bear arms against their country, to become the executioners of their friends and brethren, or to fall themselves by their hands.*
>
> *He has excited domestic insurrections amongst us, and has endeavored to bring on the inhabitants of our frontiers, the merciless Indian savages, whose known rule of warfare, is undistinguished destruction of all ages, sexes and conditions.*

The thirteen original colonies were New York, New Jersey, Pennsylvania, Connecticut, New Hampshire, Rhode Island, Delaware, Massachusetts, Virginia, Maryland, North Carolina, South Carolina, and Georgia. Military hostilities first began in Massachusetts. The Constitution was written in Philadelphia, Pennsylvania. New York, New York was the initial seat of the nation's capital. Virginia was the most populous state and home to three of America's first four presidents: George Washington, Thomas Jefferson, and James Madison. John Adams, America's second president, hailed from Massachusetts. When the colonists began to feel the strain of colonization, they organized themselves into what was known as the Continental Congress. The Continental Congress would eventually serve as the foundation for the new nation that was to form the bases of the thirteen colonies breaking away from British rule. The ***First Continental Congress*** was organized to petition the king to address a series of grievances posed by the colonies. The principal demand of the First Continental Congress was for an easing of tax burdens on the colonies. The colonists were also upset that they had no say over policies that ruled their lives. This is the context of the phrase "taxation without representation." When the colonists realized that the king would not honor any of their demands they formed the **Second Continental Congress** in order to secure an organized effort to secede from Great Britain.[1] The Congress charged Thomas Jefferson with writing a document declaring independence from Great Britain. On July 4, 1776 independence was declared. The **Declaration of Independence** became not only one the prominent documents in American political literature, but a prominent document in the sphere of revolutionary literature.

REVOLUTION

Revolution is the fundamental change in political organization; especially the overthrow or renunciation of one government or ruler and substitution of another by the governed. There are cultural revolutions, social revolutions, and political revolutions. Regardless of the area in question, revolutions evoke change and revolutions bring change. Revolutions often have a positive connotation, but their outcomes are not always positive. More often than not political revolutions are very violent affairs that are nothing short of all out warfare.

The American Revolution was not unlike other significant political revolutions that have occurred over time. They essentially have similar beginnings even if the outcomes are not the same. For example, they usually begin with a sense of alienation from the dominant power structure. This sense of alienation is based on the idea that the status quo offers no mechanism for a redress of grievances. These sentiments were echoed in Jefferson's Declaration of Independence, which is nothing less than a revolutionary manifesto:

> *When, in the course of human events, it becomes necessary for one people to dissolve the political bands which have connected them with another, and to assume among the powers of the earth, the separate and equal station to which the laws*

1 David McCullough, *John Adams* New York: Simon & Schuster Paperbacks, 2001.

of nature and of nature's God entitle them, a decent respect to the opinions of mankind requires that they should declare the causes which impel them to the separation.

We hold these truths to be self-evident, that all men are created equal, that they are endowed by their Creator with certain unalienable rights, that among these are life, liberty and the pursuit of happiness. That to secure these rights, governments are instituted among men, deriving their just powers from the consent of the governed. That whenever any form of government becomes destructive to these ends, it is the right of the people to alter or to abolish it, and to institute new government, laying its foundation on such principles and organizing its powers in such form, as to them shall seem most likely to effect their safety and happiness. Prudence, indeed, will dictate that governments long established should not be changed for light and transient causes; and accordingly all experience hath shown that mankind are more disposed to suffer, while evils are sufferable, than to right themselves by abolishing the forms to which they are accustomed. But when a long train of abuses and usurpations, pursuing invariably the same object evinces a design to reduce them under absolute despotism, it is their right, it is their duty, to throw off such government, and to provide new guards for their future security.[2]

Other important thinkers regarding the American Revolution include: Patrick Henry, Thomas Paine (author of "Common Sense"), and Samuel Adams.

The French Revolution 1789

The American Revolutionary War concluded in 1785. By the time of the French Revolution, America had begun settling in as an independent

---

2 Copyright in the Public Domain.

country. The Articles of Confederation had been replaced by the U.S. Constitution, which would soon be ratified. Washington would become America's first president under the new Constitution. His inauguration took place on April 30, 1789 against the backdrop of the French Revolution. Although the French Revolution had concluded before 1800, both Haitian Independence in 1803 and the Louisiana Purchase of 1803 are linked to revolutionary developments in France. It should be noted that Thomas Jefferson, the third president of the United States, was a French sympathizer. John Adams, the second president of the United States, was leery of the French. President Adams supported the Alien and Sedition Acts that targeted the French in the United States. Just as the American Revolution was inspired by the Declaration of Independence, the French Revolution was inspired by the Declaration of the Rights of Man. A brief excerpt follows:

> ***Declaration of the Rights of Man 1789***
>
> *The representatives of the French people, constituted into a National Assembly, considering that ignorance, forgetting or contempt of the rights of man are the sole causes of public misfortunes and of the corruption of governments, are resolved to expose, in a solemn declaration, the natural, inalienable and sacred rights of man, so that that declaration, constantly present to all members of the social body, points out to them without cease their rights and their duties; so that the acts of the legislative power and those of the executive power, being at every instant able to be compared with the goal of any political institution, are very respectful of it; so that the complaints of the citizens, founded from now on simple and incontestible principles, turn always to the maintenance of the Constitution and to the happiness of all.*
>
> *In consequence, the National Assembly recognizes and declares, in the presence and under the auspices of the Supreme Being, the following rights of man and of the citizen:*

> ***Article I**—Men are born and remain free and equal in rights. Social distinctions can be founded only on the common good.*
>
> ***Article II**—The goal of any political association is the conservation of the natural and imprescriptible rights of man. These rights are liberty, property, safety and resistance against oppression.*[3]

The Bolshevik Revolution 1917

Karl Marx published the Communist Manifesto in 1848, a full sixty-nine years before the Bolshevik Revolution. The Bolshevik Revolution ultimately led to the formation of the Soviet Union, which embodied a Marxist-Leninist Communist state. The Soviet Union became a superpower and rival to the United States. This rivalry came to be known as the Cold War. The Soviet Union collapsed in 1991.

The Chinese Revolution 1949

The Chinese Revolution was led by Mao Zedong (Mao Tse-Tung). After Mao had successfully taken power, another component of the Chinese Revolution arose: the Cultural Revolution. The Chinese Revolution occurred in 1949. The Chinese Revolution was considered an agrarian revolution. In China, land constituted the means of production as opposed to factories. China is still considered a Communist state; however, its relationship with the United States and the world is based on a capitalist format. This relationship with China has been developed over time. President Richard Nixon made the first inroads to China with a celebrated trip to China in 1972. President Jimmy Carter then followed up on the overtures to China when he announced normalization of relations in 1978.

The Cuban Revolution 1959

The Cuban Revolution brought Fidel Castro to power. It was a Communist revolution in opposition to Fulgencio Batista. It began in 1953 and concluded with the overthrow of Batista in 1959. The revolution brought about a significant change for the previous system of government. Castro was established as a dictator and held on to power until health-related issues forced him to hand over power to his brother Raul Castro. The United States has been an antagonist toward Cuba since its revolution. For example, the Bay of Pigs Invasion (a CIA operation that failed in its intended outcome of bringing down the Castro regime) was planned during the Eisenhower administration and carried out under Kennedy. Until President Obama's recent announcement concerning normalization of relations with Cuba, the country has been treated as a pariah nation by United States foreign policy. It still remains to be seen if the American Congress will pass legislation to lift sanctions and ease travel restrictions to Cuba.

The Ethiopian Revolution 1974

Ethiopia is the only original African nation that was never colonized. Haile Selassie ascended to the throne in 1930. He was referred to as the Lion From the Tribe of Judah who traces his lineage to King Solomon and the Queen of Sheba. Italy invaded Ethiopia in the 1930s with a design toward colonization but was never able to subdue the country as a whole. Selassie returned to the throne in 1941.

The Ethiopian Revolution represented the overthrow of the Imperial Monarchy of Emperor Haile Selassie. The impetus for change stemmed initially from the impact of a drought that was exacerbated by the policies of the regime. The regime had already been weakened. Selassie was in no position to put up much resistance. The forces opposing Selassie referred to themselves as the Derg. A major difference between the American Revolution and the Ethiopian Revolution is that democracy or representative democracy was not established. Although the Derg did not begin as a Marxist regime, they declared themselves a Marxist regime in 1981. This strained relations with the United States until the collapse of the Soviet Union.

The Iranian Revolution 1979

The Iranian Revolution brought down the regime of the Shah of Iran. During the revolution, the American Embassy was seized and American hostages were taken. The regime of the Shah of Iran was overthrown just as the Shah had come to power in 1949. It has been reported that the United States was instrumental in bringing the Shah to power. The Iranian Revolution and the hostage crisis were synonymous events. Not only were the U.S. hostages held captive for more than a year, but the latter part of the Carter presidency was held captive also.

The Nicaraguan Revolution 1979

The Marxist Sandinistas overthrew the dictatorship of Anastasio Somoza Debayle. The Nicaraguan Revolution ran afoul of the United States' Monroe Doctrine, which was established by President James Monroe. The Monroe Doctrine saw Central and South America as being in America's sphere of influence. America's opposition to the Sandinistas was the basis for one of the largest scandals to plague the Reagan administration. Operatives in the Reagan administration were found to have been selling weapons to Iran in order to fund destabilization efforts in Nicaragua.[4] The Marxist Regime was not overthrown but did moderate their policies.

---

4 Oliver North, *Taking the Stand*. New York: Pocket Books, 1987.

The Arab Spring 2011

Tarek al-Tayeb Mohamed Bouazizi committed self immolation on December 17, 2010. He died from his injuries on January 4, 2011. Protests ensued and by January 14, 2011 President Zine El Abidine Ben Ali of Tunisia was forced to step down from office after having been in power for twenty-three years. This was the beginning of what has become known as "The Arab Spring." At its height The Arab Spring was a movement across North Africa and the Middle East calling for long-term dictators to step down and usher in an era of democracy. In the midst of The Arab Spring the regime of Muammar Al Qaddafi in Libya fell to rebel forces aided by NATO airstrikes. In Egypt, the long-term presidency of Hosni Mubarak was toppled when throngs of Egyptians assembled in Tariq Square and refused to move until the Mubarak regime came to an end. When Mubarak stepped down, great jubilation filled the country and a democratic election followed.

Once a revolution begins, it is impossible to know where it will end or how it will develop. The rhetoric and aspirations employed to sustain a revolution can fail to be established once the new order comes to power. Many revolutions have begun with democratic inspiration only to descend into totalitarianism or authoritarianism. The American Revolution did not usher in a perfect nation. However, it laid the foundation to form a more perfect union. The flexibility of the ensuing Constitution and the flexibility of the government to change with the passage of time have contributed to the longevity of the nation. George Washington realized this when, in his Farewell Address to the nation, he admonished the nation to realize that their "government" is the source of their peace, prosperity, and happiness. Consequently, Washington warned that nothing should separate the people from their government.[5]

5 http://avalon.law.yale.edu/18th_century/washing.asp

NOTES

Horton, James Oliver and Lois E. Horton. *Slavery and the Making of America*. Oxford: Oxford University Press, 2005.

McCullough, David. *John Adams*. New York: Simon and Schuster Paperbacks, 2001.

2 THE CONSTITUTION

The current Constitution by which the United States is governed is not the nation's first governing document. The Articles of Confederation were drafted prior to the Constitution. The document was referred to as the Articles of Confederation because the nation was a loose association of thirteen independent states. The opening lines of the document read "The United States in Congress Assembled." The states created a Congress in with which to rule themselves. However, there were no "checks and balances." There was no "separation of powers." There was a president, but there was no independent executive branch. The president, under the Articles of Confederation, was selected directly by Congress. Not only was there no independent executive, there was no independent judiciary. Congress settled disputes. Congress was not only the center of the new national government, it was the national government. The essential weakness, however, of the central government was that its power was not greater than the collective state power or the power of an individual dissenting state.

The Articles of Confederation was the governing document from 1781 to 1787. There were presidents who served under the Articles of Confederation. The first was John Hanson (see Table 2.1). What becomes evident while considering Table 2.1 is that the selected presidents only served for a single, one-year term.

TABLE 2.1

PRESIDENTS UNDER THE ARTICLES OF CONFEDERATION

1.	John Hanson (1782)
2.	Elias Boudinot (1783)
3.	Thomas Mifflin (1784)
4.	Richard Henry Lee (1785)
5.	John Hancock (1786)
6.	Nathan Gorman (1787)
7.	Arthur Saint Clair (1788)
8.	Cyrus Griffin (1789)

The weakness of the national government caused alarm and led to a call for a convention in order to amend the Articles of Confederation. The Constitutional Convention began in May 1787. Major issues that needed to be settled included representation, African enslavement, and how to select or elect a president. When the Constitution was completed on September 17, 1787, the document revealed a series of compromises that were reached between major competing factions.[1] As it pertains to representation, a compromise was reached between big states and small states. The large states put forth the ***Virginia Plan***, which called for representation based on a state's population. The small states set forth the ***New Jersey Plan***, which called for equal representation. The issue was solved with the Connecticut Compromise. The Connecticut Compromise set forth a scheme of representation that could accommodate both the large states and the small states. A ***bicameral legislature*** was created for this purpose. "Bicameral" simply refers to two houses within a legislative division. In the American scheme, the upper house would be known as the Senate. The Senate would be based on equal representation by allowing each state two senators. The lower house would be known as the House of Representatives. The House of Representatives would be based on population. As outlined in Article I,

1 Kevin R. C. Gutzman, *James Madison and the Making of America. New York:* St. Martin's Press, 2012.

Section 2, Paragraph 4, "The actual Enumeration shall be made within three Years after the first Meeting of the Congress of the United States, and within every subsequent term of ten Years, in such Manner as they shall by Law direct." There would be a set number of representatives to the House of Representatives. Each state's delegation would be determined by the states population. State populations would be counted by a census that would be held every ten years.

The Constitution was created during the summer of 1787 in Philadelphia, Pennsylvania. There were fifty-five delegates representing the thirteen newly independent states. Over that summer not all fifty-five delegates were assembled at any one time. The population of the United States was just over two million. Close to 17 percent of the population were enslaved Africans. Women were essentially second-class citizens. Property ownership enabled a differentiation between the haves and the have-nots.

PRE-AMENDED CONSTITUTION: Articles I–VII

The U.S. Constitution can be divided into three essential sections. First, there is what is called The Pre-Amended Constitution. The Pre-Amended Constitution consists of the seven original Articles. This is the document that upheld the institution of enslavement. This is also the document that reflects the main interests of the framers of the Constitution. Second, there is the Bill of Rights. The Bill of Rights consists of the first ten Amendments to the Constitution. A discussion of the first ten Amendments is a discussion of civil liberties in the United States. The third major area of the Constitution is what is called the Civil War Amendments. The Civil War Amendments comprise the Thirteenth, Fourteenth, and Fifteenth Amendments.

Article I of the Constitution is the legislative article. Article I is also the most lengthy Article in the Constitution. This gives evidence that Congress, in moving away from the old Constitution, would still be a very important part of the new government. Section 1 states, "All legislative Powers herein granted shall be vested in a Congress of the United States, which shall consist of a Senate and House of Representative."

Section 2 describes the House of Representatives. Section 3 describes the Senate. Both Sections give the qualifications to be elected and serve in each House. The essential differences in each House are also detailed in Article I. For example, Section 7, Paragraph 1 gives the exclusive power of introducing revenue bills to the House of Representatives in declaring, "All Bills raising Revenue shall originate in the House of Representatives ..." One can understand why this provision was made in response to on the revolutionary principle of "taxation without representation." The framers of the Constitution thought it wise to place issues of taxation in the House, which was more closely aligned with the people. The Senate was given the exclusive power of "advice and consent" regarding treaties and confirmation of presidential appointees.

The Constitution is designed for majority rule with protection of minority rights. There is no reference to racial minority in this context. Minority in this respect applies to a numerical opinion or position. The framers of the Constitution were mindful of the class differences in society and sought to design a government that could protect liberty and place a check on the people. James Madison, who would become the third president of the United States, made this point very clearly in Federalist #10:

> *By a faction, I understand a number of citizens, whether amounting to a majority or a minority of the whole, who are united and actuated by some common impulse of passion, or of interest, adversed to the rights of other citizens, or to the permanent and aggregate interests of the community.*
>
> *There are two methods of curing the mischiefs of faction: the one, by removing its causes; the other, by controlling its effects.*
>
> *There are again two methods of removing the causes of faction: the one, by destroying the liberty which is essential to its existence; the other, by giving to every citizen the same opinions, the same passions, and the same interests.*
>
> *It could never be more truly said than of the first remedy, that it was worse than the disease. Liberty is to faction what air is*

to fire, an aliment without which it instantly expires. But it could not be less folly to abolish liberty, which is essential to political life, because it nourishes faction, than it would be to wish the annihilation of air, which is essential to animal life, because it imparts to fire its destructive agency.

The second expedient is as impracticable as the first would be unwise. As long as the reason of man continues fallible, and he is at liberty to exercise it, different opinions will be formed. As long as the connection subsists between his reason and his self-love, his opinions and his passions will have a reciprocal influence on each other; and the former will be objects to which the latter will attach themselves. The diversity in the faculties of men, from which the rights of property originate, is not less an insuperable obstacle to a uniformity of interests. The protection of these faculties is the first object of government. From the protection of different and unequal faculties of acquiring property, the possession of different degrees and kinds of property immediately results; and from the influence of these on the sentiments and views of the respective proprietors, ensues a division of the society into different interests and parties.

The latent causes of faction are thus sown in the nature of man; and we see them everywhere brought into different degrees of activity, according to the different circumstances of civil society. A zeal for different opinions concerning religion, concerning government, and many other points, as well of speculation as of practice; an attachment to different leaders ambitiously contending for pre-eminence and power; or to persons of other descriptions whose fortunes have been interesting to the human passions, have, in turn, divided mankind into parties, inflamed them with mutual animosity, and rendered them much more disposed to vex and oppress each other than to co-operate for their common good. So strong is this propensity of mankind to fall into mutual animosities, that where no substantial occasion presents itself, the most frivolous and fanciful distinctions have been sufficient to kindle their unfriendly passions and excite their most violent conflicts. But the most common and durable source of factions has been the various and unequal distribution of property. Those who hold and those who are without property have ever formed distinct interests in society. Those who are creditors, and those who are debtors, fall under a like discrimination. A landed interest, a manufacturing interest, a mercantile interest, a moneyed interest, with many lesser interests, grow up of necessity in civilized nations, and divide them into different classes, actuated by different sentiments and views. The regulation of these various and interfering interests forms the principal task of modern legislation, and involves the spirit of party and faction in the necessary and ordinary operations of the government.[2]

The U.S. Senate initially contained one of these safeguards against democracy. Prior to the ratification of the Seventeenth Amendment in 1913, U.S. senators were elected by state legislatures. Therefore, when thinking about Senate elections prior to 1917, one should be mindful of this reality. For example, when Abraham Lincoln lost his Senate bid to Stephen Douglass, he lost it in the state legislature, not in a statewide vote of the people. Lincoln basically carried the northern parts of Illinois. Douglass was stronger in the southern part of the state. The southern delegation was more influenced by the southern states that were wary of Lincoln and the Republican Party.

Article II of the Constitution is the Executive Article. It reflects the reality that the framers chose to have a single executive that would be subject to the "checks and balances" of Congress and the Supreme Court. As stated in Article II, "The executive Power shall be vested in a President of the United States of America. He shall hold his Office during the Term of four Years." One should notice immediately a change that has come to the presidency since it was created in 1787. The president's term is still four years, but the president has been limited to two terms. George Washington, the nation's first president under the

2 James Madison, from "Federalist #10," *The Federalist Papers*. Copyright in the Public Domain.

new Constitution, served two four-year terms. A two-term maximum became presidential custom until the presidency of Franklin Roosevelt. Roosevelt was elected to four consecutive terms. The two-elected term maximum was made constitutional by the Twenty-second Amendment. The maximum time that an individual can serve as president is ten years. This came close to being demonstrated when Johnson took over after Kennedy was assassinated. There was just over a year left in Kennedy's first term when he was assassinated. Johnson finished out Kennedy's first term and was elected to the presidency in 1964. He was eligible to run again in 1968 but chose not to seek reelection due to the mounting troubles in Vietnam.

Article II also contains the method by which the president would be chosen. The method by which the president would be chosen was one of the essential compromises made in order to bring the new government into existence. The compromise came to be known as the ***Electoral College***. The Electoral College is another check on democratic impulses. The framers removed the election of the president from the people and placed it with electors from each state. Although in today's political culture citizens go to polls in order to cast a ballot, it is actually the electors who elect the president of the United States.

The next very important compromise that had to be reached in order to bring the new nation into existence was the compromise over African enslavement. The fact that the Constitution contains the actual results of the negotiations over enslavement gives evidence of the weight and gravity concerning the institution of African enslavement. The agreements that were reached are directly linked to the Civil War Amendments, which reversed African enslavement provisions in the Constitution. There were three essential compromises that were reached over the issue enslavement. African enslavement had existed in the North American colonies for more than 168 years prior to the writing of the Constitution. The institution of African enslavement continued for another eighty-three years before the Thirteenth Amendment brought about the reversal of the legal sanctioning of African enslavement. The African enslavement compromises are as follows:

> ***1. Article I, Section 2, Paragraph 3:*** *Representatives and direct Taxes shall be apportioned among the several States which may*

be included within this Union, according to their respective Numbers, which shall be determined by adding to the whole Number of free Persons, including those bound to Service for a Term of Years, and excluding Indians not taxed, three fifths of all other Persons.

2. Article I, Section 9, Paragraph 1: *The Migration or Importation of such Persons as any of the States now existing shall think proper to admit, shall not be prohibited by the Congress prior to the Year one thousand eight hundred and eight, but a Tax or duty may be imposed on such Importation, not exceeding ten dollars for each Person.*

3. Article IV, Section 2, Paragraph 3: *No Person held to Service or Labour in one State, under the Laws thereof, escaping into another, shall, in Consequence of any Law or Regulation therein, be discharged from such Service or Labour, but shall be delivered up on Claim of the Party to whom such Service or Labour may be due.*[3]

Article I, Section 2, Paragraph 3 is known as the "3/5 clause." Popular belief states that Africans were seen as 3/5 of a person. This is a misconception of the 3/5 clause. The enslaved Africans were not seen as humans. They were known to be human, but they were not seen as human. The Africans were seen as property. They were seen as cattle with no higher status than a beast of the field. The 3/5 Compromise was a formula for counting the Africans who had been enslaved for the purpose of increasing the southern planters' strength in Congress and the Electoral College. The southern planters wanted to count the entire population given the proliferation of Africans in the south. This is not to say that enslavement did not exist above the Mason-Dixon Line, yet the majority of those who were enslaved were found in the south. In some communities the African population outnumbered the white population. Therefore the compromise was to allow the southern planters to count 3/5 of the population. For example, for every 100

3 Copyright in the Public Domain.

Africans, 60 could be counted toward the southern planters' state population.

Article I, Section 9, Paragraph 1 dealt with what was known as the "slave trade." This compromise allowed the trade of Africans to continue for another twenty years from the writing of the Constitution. The Constitution refers to "migration or importation of Such Persons." However, the trade was about importation not migration. Migration refers to the willful entrance of a people into a host country. Importation refers to products in the context of international trade. To mention the word importation in the same clause with the Africans is also evidence that the Africans were known to be human but thought of as property in the same vein as inanimate objects. This point was brought front and center in the Dred Scott Decision of 1857, which declared that black people could not be citizens under the Constitution. Justice Roger Taney, writing for the majority, stated the following:

> *A free negro of the African race, whose ancestors were brought to this country and sold as slaves, is not a "citizen" within the meaning of the Constitution of the United States.*
>
> *When the Constitution was adopted, they were not regarded in any of the States as members of the community which constituted the State, and were not numbered among its "people or citizens." Consequently, the special rights and immunities guarantied to citizens do not apply to them. And not being "citizens" within the meaning of the Constitution, they are not entitled to sue in that character in a court of the United States, and the Circuit Court has not jurisdiction in such a suit.*
>
> *Every citizen has a right to take with him into the Territory any article of property which the Constitution of the United States recognises as property.*
>
> *4. The Constitution of the United States recognises slaves as property, and pledges the Federal Government to protect it. And Congress cannot exercise any more authority over*

property of that description than it may constitutionally exercise over property of any other kind.

5. The act of Congress, therefore, prohibiting a citizen of the United States from Page 60 U. S. 396 taking with him his slaves when he removes to the Territory in question to reside is an exercise of authority over private property which is not warranted by the Constitution, and the removal of the plaintiff by his owner to that Territory gave him no title to freedom.

The words "people of the United States" and "citizens" are synonymous terms, and mean the same thing. They both describe the political body who, according to our republican institutions, form the sovereignty and who hold the power and conduct the Government through their representatives. They are what we familiarly call the "sovereign people," and every citizen is one of this people, and a constituent member of this sovereignty. The question before us is whether the class of persons described in the plea in abatement compose a portion of this people, and are constituent members of this sovereignty? We think they are not, and that they are not included, and were not intended to be included, under the word "citizens" in the Constitution, and can therefore claim none of the rights and privileges which that instrument provides for and secures to citizens of the United States. On the contrary, they were at that time considered as a subordinate and inferior class of beings who had been subjugated by the dominant race, and, whether emancipated or not, yet remained subject to their authority, and had no rights or privileges but such as those who held the power and the Government might choose to grant them.

The language of the Declaration of Independence is equally conclusive:

It begins by declaring that,

"[w]hen in the course of human events it becomes necessary for one people to dissolve the political bands which have connected them with another, and to assume among the powers of the earth the separate and equal station to which the laws of nature and nature's God entitle them, a decent respect for the opinions of mankind requires that they should declare the causes which impel them to the separation."

It then proceeds to say:

"We hold these truths to be self-evident: that all men are created equal; that they are endowed by their Creator with certain unalienable rights; that among them is life, liberty, and the pursuit of happiness; that to secure these rights, Governments are instituted, deriving their just powers from the consent of the governed."

The general words above quoted would seem to embrace the whole human family, and if they were used in a similar instrument at this day would be so understood. But it is too clear for dispute that the enslaved African race were not intended to be included, and formed no part of the people who framed and adopted this declaration, for if the language, as understood in that day, would embrace them, the conduct of the distinguished men who framed the Declaration of Independence would have been utterly and flagrantly inconsistent with the principles they asserted, and instead of the sympathy of mankind to which they so confidently appealed, they would have deserved and received universal rebuke and reprobation.

Yet the men who framed this declaration were great men—high in literary acquirements, high in their sense of honor, and incapable of asserting principles inconsistent with those on which they were acting. They perfectly understood the meaning of the language they used, and how it would be understood by others, and they knew that it would not in any part of the civilized world be supposed to embrace the negro race,

> *which, by common consent, had been excluded from civilized Governments and the family of nations, and doomed to slavery. They spoke and acted according to the then established doctrines and principles, and in the ordinary language of the day, and no one misunderstood them. The unhappy black race were separated from the white by indelible marks, and laws long before established, and were never thought of or spoken of except as property, and when the claims of the owner or the profit of the trader were supposed to need protection.*[4]

The Dred Scott Decision sealed the fate of the United States in terms of the debate surrounding African enslavement. The decision signaled that the original intent of the Founders of the nation was that African enslavement was to continue ad infinitum. This decision coupled with the election of Abraham Lincoln as president proved that the nation could not last under the weight of trying to live "half slave and half free." The Civil War began as southern states, led by South Carolina, began to secede from the Union. The Civil War was a long and bloody resulting in the Union forces winning out over the secessionists states. The roughly twelve year Reconstruction period followed.

Article IV, Section 2, Paragraph 3 of the Constitution provided for the return of Africans who tried to flee enslavement. In general, Article IV of the Constitution, as part of the first seven Articles, sought to define relations between the states. Under the Articles of the Confederation, the states were ***sovereign*** entities. Therefore, Article IV meant to establish equality among the states. A major component of Article IV is the "full faith and credit" clause. Full faith and credit is the sinew that binds the states together in a bond of mutual respect. It should be remembered that the Africans were thought of as property. The "full faith and credit" aspect would be recognized by the state to which the Africans had fled when that state facilitated the return of requested property. This aspect remains a feature of relations between the states as it pertains to extraditions in the criminal justice system. Two laws were passed during enslavement that helpe to bolster Article

4 Justice Roger B. Taney, from The Dred Scott Decision of 1857. Copyright in the Public Domain.

IV, Section 1, Paragraph 1. The first law was the Fugitive Slave Law of 1793. The second law was the Fugitive Slave Law of 1850. Coming only six years after the Constitution was written, the Fugitive Slave Law of 1793 provides evidence that the institution of enslavement was problematic. It was difficult to hold human beings as property. This law was passed early in George Washington's second term in office. Nevertheless, this did not stem the tide of individuals seeking to escape the bonds of enslavement. Consequently, there was a second Fugitive Slave Law passed in 1850. Millard Fillmore signed the law after having been president for less than three months. The 1850 law sought to strengthen the 1793 law by imposing fines and penalties on anyone, including law enforcement officials, who did not arrest fugitive Africans who sought freedom by escaping enslavement. This law, along with the Supreme Court Decision, added to tensions between pro-enslavement forces and anti-enslavement forces.

Article V of the Pre-Amended Constitution describes how the Constitution could be amended. Amendments could be proposed in two different methods. Two-thirds of Congress or two-thirds of the states could propose amendments to the Constitution. If proposals are adopted, it would then take three-fourths of state legislatures or three-fourths of state Conventions. Article V also contributed to the debate over enslavement, however due to the article's prohibition against curtailing the international trade of Africans until 1808. Therefore, the trade could not even be amended out of existence. Article V also ensured that the institution could not be taxed out of existence by stating that no "capitation tax" could be imposed.

THE BILL OF RIGHTS

The debate of the scope and size of the government was a major issue during the writing of the Constitution. The anti-Federalists argued that government should be limited. By limiting the power of the federal government, more power should be given to the states. The Federalists argued that the central government needed to be strong and vigorous. The Bill of Rights was a compromise between the Federalists and anti-Federalists (the Bill of Rights is discussed in more detail in the chapter on Civil Liberties.) The Bill of Rights consists of the first ten Amendments to the Constitution.

> ***First Amendment:*** *Freedom of speech, the press, religion, of assembly, to petition the government for a redress of grievances.*
>
> ***Second Amendment:*** *Right to bear arms.*
>
> ***Third Amendment:*** *Freedom from quartering soldiers.*
>
> ***Fourth Amendment:*** *Freedom from unreasonable searches and seizures.*
>
> ***Five Amendment:*** *Right to due process of law not to self-incriminate.*
>
> ***Sixth Amendment:*** *Right to counsel.*
>
> ***Seventh Amendment:*** *Right to a trial by jury*
>
> ***Eight Amendment:*** *Freedom from cruel and unusual punishment*
>
> ***Ninth Amendment:*** *Rights retained by the people*
>
> ***Tenth Amendment:*** *Rights retained by states or the people*[5]

Beyond the pre-Amended Constitution and the Bill of Rights, the Constitution began moving toward a more democratic stance and equality. The inability to end enslavement during the writing of the Constitution eventually led to the Civil War. After the Civil War there were three amendments to the Constitution that are collectively known as the ***Civil War Amendments***. The Thirteenth Amendment brought about an end to chattel enslavement. Yet, upon closer inspection, the

5 Copyright in the Public Domain.

"except clause" in the Thirteenth Amendment stated that involuntary servitude could be imposed as punishment for a crime. It can be argued that the Thirteenth Amendment transported the institution of enslavement into the criminal justice system. The rise of chain gangs and the practice of loaning out prisoners provide evidence of this development. Nevertheless, the Thirteenth Amendment brought about an appeal of the Fugitive Slave Act. The Fourteenth Amendment reversed the Dred Scott Decision. It provided for citizenship. The Dred Scott Decision ruled that blacks were not citizens and had no rights under the Constitution. In addition to providing for citizenship, the Fourteenth Amendment provided for equal protection under the law. The "equality" that Jefferson spoke of as a principle in the Declaration of Independence had been codified into the Constitution. The Fifteenth Amendment expanded the voting franchise to black men in particular and declared that no one could be denied the vote on the basis of race.

NOTES

Holton, Woody. Unruly Americans and the Origins of the Constitution. New York: Hill and Wang, 2007.

Beard, Charles. An Economic Interpretation of the Constitution. New York: MacMillan, 1913.

3 FEDERALISM

America's government is not only structured in the more understood ***separation of powers***, but in what is called ***division of power***. Whereas separation of powers refers to dispersion of executive, legislative, and judicial power among three separate branches, division of power refers to powers between federal/national government and the states. Articles I, II, and III of the Constitution address separation of powers. Federalism is addressed in Article IV and the Ninth and Tenth Amendments to the Constitution.

Article IV of the Constitution seeks to regulate behavior between the states. Key provisions include Section 1, Full Faith and Credit, and Section 2, Privileges and Immunities. Full Faith and Credit seeks to require states to honor documents and agreements that parties enter into in another state. Privileges and Immunities seek to prohibit states from discriminating against citizens of other states. This clause also addresses extradition between states. Unlike an international setting in which governments must establish extradition treaties in order to force or persuade other countries to return fugitives, the Constitution provided for extradition in order to foster unity among the states. The example of the NSA leaker, Edward Snowden, is a case in point. Russia, having no extradition treaty with the United States, did not see it as advancing their interests to return Snowden from Russia to the United States. The states, on the other hand, are governed by the Constitution, which reads in Article IV, Section 2: "A

Person charged in any State with Treason, Felony, or other Crime, who shall flee from Justice, and be found in another State, shall on Demand of the executive authority of the State from which he fled, be delivered up, to be removed to the State having Jurisdiction of the Crime." This section of the Constitution was also used to uphold the institution of African enslavement by proving that any enslaved African who had escaped captivity in one state had to be returned to the state from which they had escaped. This provision of the Constitution was bolstered by the Fugitive Slave laws of 1796 and 1850. These laws became null and void with ratification of the Thirteenth Amendment to the Constitution. The Thirteenth Amendment brought a qualified end to involuntary servitude in the United States. Those who were convicted of a crime could still face involuntary servitude. Moreover, as a convicted criminal they would be subject to Section 2, Paragraph 2 involving extradition.

Another area of the Constitution that establishes federalism is Article VI of the Constitution. Article VI, Paragraph 2 states, "This Constitution, and the Laws of the United States which shall be made Pursuance thereof; and all Treaties made, or which shall be made, under Authority of the United States, shall be the supreme Law of the Land; and the Judges in every State shall be bound thereby." Although the national government and the states share power and draw legitimacy from the Constitution, the laws of the federal government are indeed the supreme law of the land. Consequently, state law, in addition to federal law, has to conform to the Constitution. Both the Ninth and the Tenth Amendments address the shared power aspect of the state and federal governments. The Ninth Amendment essentially looks at the rights of the people residing in states. The Tenth Amendment explicitly denotes shared powers between the states and the federal government by stating, "The powers not delegated to the United States by the Constitution, nor prohibited by it to the States, are reserved to the States respectively, or to the people." It has been argued by some that the Ninth Amendment serves as part of the basis for the idea of a right to privacy. This aspect will be fully addressed in Chapter 4.

Using Madison's Federalist #10 as a guide, one can see that many aspects of the American political system are designed along lines the federal system that constitute a republican form of government over a democratic form of government. The following serve as examples:

***The Electoral College*:** The Electoral College was designed as a method of electing the president of the United States. The electors are elected on a state-by-state basis. Given the reality of America's two-party system, each state selects two slates of electors. Whatever party wins a particular state wins that state's electors. The number of electors is determined by a state's Congressional delegation (two senators plus members of the House) and three electors are assigned to Washington, D.C., making a total of 538 electors.

***The Federal Court System*:** The federal court system is also designed around the federal system of government. There are thirteen Circuit Courts of Appeal based on thirteen circuits that cut across state lines. This layer of the federal court system was establish by the Judiciary Act of 1869. There are ninety four District Courts. This includes one in the District of Columbia and one in Puerto Rico. The district courts are the courts of original jurisdiction or trial courts. The ninety-four districts are analogous to the 435 congressional districts.

***The Federal Reserve System*:** The Federal Reserve System is another governmental institution set up along the lines of federalism. The Federal Reserve (The Fed) was created in 1913. The Fed has three levels with three distinct functions. First, there is the Federal Reserve Board. The Board consists of the Chair and Vice Chair. The Federal Open Market Committee (FOMC) is the main policy making component of The Fed. It consists of the Board of Governors and Reserve Bank Presidents. There are also twelve regions associated with the Federal Reserve. Although The Fed was created in 1913, it is not the first national bank. The issue of a national bank was first raised by Alexander Hamilton. Consequently, the first national bank of the United States was chartered in 1791 for twenty years. The charter of the First Bank of the United States was allowed to expire under the Jefferson administration. Jefferson had initially been opposed to the bank. War debt from the War of 1812 gave impetus for chartering the Second Bank of the United States 1816–1836. Issues surrounding federalism and the national bank were settled in McCulloch v. Maryland 1819. The state of Maryland wanted to tax the bank. However, the Supreme Court ruled that a state entity could not tax a federal entity thus reaffirming national supremacy. According to the Court, "the power to tax is the power to destroy." Nevertheless, President Jackson, a southern Democrat who was opposed to a national bank, allowed the charter to lapse. It was not until the Federal Reserve was created in 1913 that another national bank was attempted.

PUBLIC POLITICAL PRACTICE AND FEDERALISM

One of the consequences of the American federal system is a certain unevenness of public political practice. Despite the "full faith and credit" clause different states are allowed to have different practices until the Supreme Court settles a national question about a particular issue. For example, in Brown v. Board of Education, the Supreme Court ruled that school segregation and the concept of separate but equal were unconstitutional. The national settlement of this issue was reaffirmed in Cooper v. Aaron 1958. The Court stated that although Brown was decided on a Kansas-based case, the ruling had national implications. The following represent public political practice issues that vary or have the potential to vary from state to state.

1. ***Same-Sex Marriage***: The state of Hawaii recently legalized same-sex marriage. It became the sixteenth state to allow same-sex marriage. Ironically, it was Hawaii that visited the issue in the 1990s. This is what prompted Congress to pass the Marriage Protection Act of 1996. According to this law "marriage is defined as the union between one man and one woman." An attempt to circumvent the "full faith and credit" clause is what prompted Congress to pass the legislation. Although the legislation was conservative, it was signed into law by President Bill Clinton. Same-sex marriage has a long and complicated narrative. Similar to African Americans initially being seen as property, the ontological reality of homosexuality first had to be seen as a human reality that was not meant to be set inside the realm of constitutional protection. In Bowers v. Hardwick 1986, the Supreme Court ruled

that state sodomy laws were constitutional because local communities should have the power to regulate their moral community standards. At the time of this particular ruling, there were about twenty-six states that banned the practice of sodomy. Once again, the unevenness of state public political practice was quite apparent. How could marriage between two couples of the same sex be constitutional if love and sex between these couples were outlawed as an abomination before God? The Supreme Court reversed its course in Lawrence v. Texas 2003 by ruling that state sodomy laws were unconstitutional. This ruling set the table for major state-to-state battles over the issue of same-sex marriage. None was more contentious than the California referendum on whether to outlaw same sex marriage. Proposition 8 was successful in amending the California constitution in order to ban gay marriage. Ironically, this amendment was ratified by the people of California on the same night that Barack Obama was elected President. President Obama campaigned on the ideal of civil unions and was initially opposed to same-sex marriage. It was not until after the election of 2012 that President Obama came to publicly support same-sex marriage. He also stated that his administration would not support the 1996 Defense of Marriage Act.[1] The cause of same-sex marriage was further advanced in 2013 when the Defense of Marriage Act was found unconstitutional in United States v. Windsor. Proposition 8 was returned to the state of California, thus rendering a lower court's injunction against the enactment of Proposition 8 as the last ruling on the proposition. The ruling in Windsor coupled with the current position of Proposition 8 makes the issue of same-sex marriage similar to that of the death penalty. Some states allow same-sex marriage while other states do not allow same-sex marriage. What is unsettled is the question as to whether states that do not allow same-sex marriage must honor such unions from other states under the "full faith and credit" clause of Article IV of the Constitution. Until such time as the Court rules on a national question of state practice regarding same-sex marriage, same-sex couples who marry will have to live in a legal limbo as far as state laws are concerned. One can only imagine how life would be if Jim Crow segregation laws were allowed to continue in a similar

1 www.cbsnews.com/news/obama-administration-will-no-longer-defend-doma

manner with some states allowed to practice Jim Crow while others chose not to engage in the practice.

2. ***The Death Penalty*:** As mentioned above, the death penalty is another area of uneven practice from state to state. The Supreme Court ruled the death penalty unconstitutional in the 1972 case Furman v. Georgia only to reverse itself four years later in Gregg v. Georgia. Currently the death penalty is constitutional, yet states do not have to impose the death penalty. Simply stated, one's chances of getting the death penalty for committing murder rests on which state has jurisdiction. For example, the state of New York placed a halt on its death penalty, while states such as Texas put many inmates to death.

3. ***The Legal Drinking Age*:** Mothers Against Driving Drunk (MADD) was very instrumental in having the legal drinking age raised to twenty-one from eighteen years of age. Although the states were not required to raise their legal drinking age to twenty-one, a major incentive was given in the way of forfeiting millions in highway funds for noncompliance. As of this writing, all fifty states adhere to the twenty-one-year old minimum legal drinking age.

4. ***State Speed Limits*:** The 1973 oil embargo on the part of the Organization of Petroleum Exporting Countries (OPEC) created a major energy crisis in the United States that lasted well into the Carter administration, prompting President Carter to call the energy crisis "the moral equivalent of war." President Carter also signed the Department of Energy into existence in 1977. A few years before Carter took Office, Congress acting in 1974 established the fifty-five mile-per-hour speed limit on a national level. Highway funds were based on a state's compliance with the law. The law had a two-fold purpose. First, it was meant to curtail energy consumption by reducing America's dependence on oil imports. Second, it was stated that the lower speeds would save lives and reduce accidents on the nation's highways. Based on new studies, safer cars, and state resistance to the law, it was repealed in 1995. Each state is once again in control

of road speeds in respective states. Due to this, one may encounter an array of speed limits driving from state to state.

PRESIDENTIAL MODELS OF PUBLIC POLITICAL PRACTICE AND FEDERALISM

***Cooperative Federalism*:** Franklin Roosevelt's New Deal was known as "Cooperative Federalism." Cooperative federalism attempted to establish joint domestic ventures between the president and the states. This was a major feature of Roosevelt's New Deal. States would assist in running federally mandated programs that were essentially created as part of the New Deal. The states would also assist in funding. This was a major restructuring of the federal arrangements that were designed to deliver more services to the people of the various states.

***Creative Federalism*:** In a commencement address to the University of Michigan, Lyndon Johnson proposed his Great Society, which also came to be known as the "War on Poverty." Lyndon Johnson's federal arrangement was known as "Creative Federalism." This was a major feature of the Great Society or War on Poverty. The purpose was to make sure that federal monies would address what Johnson saw as the issue of poverty in America. Creative federalism would utilize categorical grants in order to designate where federal funds had to be applied. In some cases, Johnson would bypass state legislatures and city councils altogether in order to make federal funds directly available to the people. This was an essential part of Johnson's antipoverty program. It was also a tool that was used in order to secure the movement of the Black constituency from Republicans to Democrats.

***New Federalism*:** Richard Nixon's new federalism was a conservative answer to the New Deal and Johnson's Great Society. Nixon argued that fewer regulations meant less government and more power to the states to decide where to apply government funding. It had a state's rights component in that it promoted revenue sharing and block grants over categorical grants. A categorical grant is money from the federal government that has to be spent according to federal guidelines and purposes. With the passage of the Revenue Sharing Act of 1972, Nixon promoted what was called "free money" from the federal government due the lack of restrictions on how the money could be spent. This was money that was channeled to state governments in order for those entities to determine where the funds would be applied. Johnson had tried to divert money directly to urban communities due to suburban and rural dominance in the state houses. Consequently, urban areas would not be short changed.

New Federalism **(Reagan):** Ronald Reagan's version of new federalism was rhetorically similar to the Nixon's new federalism. Reagan's additional emphasis on deficit reduction, however, caused his new federalism to differ, in practice, from Nixon's new federalism. Reagan also believed that states should have more autonomy. In his First Inaugural Address, President Reagan stated that "government is not the solution; government is the problem." Shrinking the scope and reach of government was Reagan's way of getting government "off the backs of the people." Consequently, Reagan believed that the states should not only have more autonomy, but that they should also have the responsibility of funding those areas where they still wanted to provide services.

***Obamacare*:** The Affordable Health Care Act of 2010 was one of President Obama's signature achievements. Its purpose was to extend healthcare to a greater number of citizens. The national government would assist in funding to the states as they set up state insurance exchanges and expanded Medicaid. The state exchanges are where private insurance providers would compete for customers at competitive rates. Federal regulation would also determine minimum standards for the insurance providers to follow.

NOTES

www.federalreserve.gov
www.energy.gov
www.uscourts.gov

4 THE SUPREME COURT

Article III of the Constitution addresses the third aspect of separation of powers and checks and balances by addressing the judicial power of the U.S. government. Article III, Section 1 states: "The judicial Power of the United States, shall be vested in one supreme Court, and in such inferior Courts as the Congress may from time to time ordain and establish. The Judges, both of the supreme and inferior Courts, shall hold their Offices during good Behavior, and shall, at stated Times, receive for their Services a Compensation which shall not be diminished during their Continuance in Office." The phrase "as the Congress may from time to time ordain and establish" solidifies the fact that Congress establishes the framework for the Supreme Court as well as the other federal courts. For example, in 1869 with the Judiciary Act, Congress established the current size of the Supreme Court at nine justices. Another example is that in 1978 Congress passed the Federal Intelligence Surveillance Act in order to address abuses of the intelligence community. A special court was established for the purpose of granting surveillance warrants to the federal government. The FISA Court came to the forefront during the accusations of the Bush Administration's warrantless surveillance.

Alexander Hamilton made a significant observation of the Supreme Court in Federalist #78. It was Hamilton's argument that the Constitution was a matter of law. Consequently, the

Supreme Court was best positioned to render an interpretation of the Constitution or reveal its meaning. Hamilton wrote: "The interpretation of the laws is the proper and peculiar province of the courts. A constitution is, in fact, and must be regarded by the judges, as a fundamental law. It therefore belongs to them to ascertain its meaning, as well as the meaning of any particular act proceeding from the legislative body. If there should happen to be an irreconcilable variance between the two, that which has the superior obligation and validity ought, of course, to be preferred; or, in other words, the Constitution ought to be preferred to the statute, the intention of the people to the intention of their agents." Hamilton's argument also was a precursor to the establishment of judicial review. Judicial review is the power of the Supreme Court to declare laws of Congress, the states, and actions of the executive unconstitutional. The Supreme Court also has the power to reverse decisions of an earlier court. Judicial review was established in the 1803 case Marbury v. Madison. The case has a political background involving the Federalists and Democratic Republican political parties. Although Hamilton is considered the founder of the Federalists and Thomas Jefferson was considered the founder of the Democratic Republicans, the Marbury case was a battle between Jefferson's legacy and the legacy of John Adams. In the larger scheme of things it turned out to be a battle between Jefferson and the legacy of the Federalists Party. It was not known in 1803 that Adams would be the last Federalists president. Chief Justice Marshall would be the standard bearer for Federalists based on Court decisions that had a strong central government bent.

The decision in Marbury v. Madison had a strong central government bias. It established the power of judicial review when it declared the Judiciary Act of 1789 unconstitutional because it gave power to the Supreme Court beyond the power bestowed upon it by the Constitution. Jefferson's challenge to the national authority of the Court proved ineffectual. Adam's legacy and the Federalist legacy would be preserved through a Federalist dominated Court.

Another case that advanced the cause of a strong central government was McCollough v. Maryland. This case yielded the famous phrase "the power to tax is the power to destroy." The state of Maryland wanted to tax the national bank of the United States. The ruling in this case continued the Federalist aim of a strong central government that ruled supreme over the states. Chief Justice Marshall would remain on the Court for another thirty-two years beyond the Marbury v. Madison decision. Roger B. Taney, the justice who would follow Marshall, made a marked departure from Marshall's Federalist positions. Taney was appointed by Democrat Andrew Jackson upon Marshall's retirement from the Court. In contrast to the Marshall Court, the Taney Court had more of a penchant for states' rights.

There are two additional concepts that are important when assessing the Court: judicial activism and judicial restraint. Judicial activism has traditionally been assigned to liberal courts, justices, and decisions. The traditional definition of judicial activism refers to judge-made law. This is the idea that judges decide cases based on a social agenda of what "ought" to be. The most notable activist court is the one lead by Chief Justice Earl Warren. Former Governor of California Earl Warren was appointed by President Dwight Eisenhower and served as chief justice from 1953 until 1969. During Earl Warren's tenure the Court handed down many decisions that continue to shape jurisprudence. Consequently, judicial activism has been heavily associated with the liberal Warren Court.

Significant Decisions Delivered by the Warren Court

1. Brown v. Board of Education
2. Cooper v. Aaron
3. Miranda v. Arizona
4. Gideon v. Wainwright
5. Engel v. Vitale
6. Griswold v. Connecticut
7. Abington v. Schempp
8. Heart of Atlanta Motel v. United States
9. Loving v. Virginia

THE WARREN COURT

Chief Justice Earl Warren, Dwight D. Eisenhower
Tom Clark, Harry Truman
Stanley Forman Reed, Franklin Roosevelt
Robert H. Jackson, Franklin Roosevelt
Harold Hitz Burton, Harry S. Truman
Sherman Minton, Harry S. Truman
Charles Evans Whittaker, Dwight Eisenhower
Potter Stewart, Dwight Eisenhower
Byron White, John F. Kennedy
William J. Brennan, Jr., Dwight D. Eisenhower
William O. Douglas, Franklin Roosevelt
Hugo Black, Franklin Roosevelt
Arthur J. Goldberg, John F. Kennedy
Felix Frankfurter, Franklin Roosevelt
Abe Fortas, Lyndon Johnson
John Marshall Harlan II, Dwight Eisenhower
Thurgood Marshall, Lyndon Johnson

Critics of the Warren Court say that school desegregation should have been settled community by community as opposed to a sweeping ruling from the Supreme Court. Such a decision is termed "judge-made law." Contemporary conservatives also look on the Warren Court with disdain due to the Court's rulings on religion, particularly in reference to bible reading and school prayer. The Roberts Court has been more of a restrained Court as it relates to these particular issues. However, given the fact that the Roberts Court has been in existence less time than the Warren Court existed, it is possible that the Court may shift based on appointments. This is particularly true with each new presidential election.

Significant Decisions Delivered by the Roberts Court

1. Citizens United v. Federal Election Commission (FEC)
2. Shelby County v. Holder
3. National Federation of Independent Business v. Sebelius
4. Windsor v. United States
5. District of Columbia v. Heller
6. Parker v. District of Columbia
7. McDonald v. Chicago
8. Burwell v. Hobby Lobby

THE ROBERTS COURT

Chief Justice John Roberts, George W. Bush
Antonin Scalia, Ronald Reagan
Anthony Kennedy, Ronald Reagan
Samuel Alito, George W. Bush
Clarence Thomas, George H. W. Bush
Sonia Sotomayor, Barack Obama
Ruth Bader Ginsberg, Bill Clinton
Elena Kagan, Barack Obama
Stephen Breyer, Bill Clinton

Judicial restraint has been associated with a conservative perspective on the Court. The philosophy of judicial restraint contends that Court decisions should be argued on the basis of the "original intent" of the writers of the Constitution. According to this perspective, if a right is not expressly or literally stated in the Constitution, it is not the place of the Court to legislate from the bench or offer interpretive constitutional amendments. Advocates of judicial restraint and original intent state that the framers offered the legislative process in order to change laws and the amendment process in order to bring about changes to the Constitution. A major area of "activist" opinion that conservatives oppose is the idea of a right to privacy in the Constitution. According to those who support "original intent," the right to privacy expressed in the Constitution does come anywhere close the rights expressed in the pre-amended Constitution or those expressed in the Bill of Rights and subsequent Amendments. Liberal jurists have basically constructed a right to privacy from the following portions of the Bill of Rights:

> ***3rd Amendment:*** *"No quartering of soldiers in peacetime without owner's consent;"*
>
> ***4th Amendment:*** *"The right of the people to be secure in persons, houses, papers, and effects against unreasonable searches and seizures..."*
>
> ***5th Amendment:*** *"Nor be deprived of life, liberty, or property, without due process of law."*
>
> ***9th Amendment:*** *"The enumeration in the Constitution of certain rights shall not be construed to deny or disparage others retained by the people."*

Significant cases involved in the construction of a right to privacy include Griswold v Connecticut 1965; Loving v. Virginia 1968; Roe v. Wade 1973; and Lawrence v. Texas 2003. Griswold v. Connecticut involved state law prohibiting the purchase and distribution of contraceptives. Loving v. Virginia dealt with state prohibitions against interracial marriages. Roe v. Wade established the constitutional right of a woman to have an abortion. Lawrence v. Texas invalidated state sodomy laws by reversing an earlier Supreme Court decision in Bowers v. Hardwick 1986, which upheld state sodomy laws.

The Roberts Court has established a reputation for being a conservative Court. This is due in part to the opinions of its most conservative justices: Antonin Scalia and Clarence Thomas. For the most part, there has been a conservative tendency from the Roberts Court; however, there have been some surprisingly liberal-leaning rulings. While voting rights have suffered under the Roberts Court, homosexual interests and same-sex marriage supporters have experienced and expansion of rights. Gun control advocates have also seen their efforts muted by the Roberts Court given the propensity of the Court to expand Second

Amendment freedoms. The most historic surprise emanating from the Roberts Court was the upholding of the Affordable Care Act. The swing vote in this decision came from Chief Justice Roberts. Many conservatives felt that this case would deal a fatal blow to the Affordable Care Act. However, the law was upheld not on the commerce clause (as supporters of the law had hoped), but on the power of Congress to tax. With the Court gradually allowing same-sex marriage to spread from state to state it would appear that this is a conservative court that is willing to uphold the right to privacy. Yet, many are skeptical of the Roberts Court given the gradual erosion of abortion rights on the part of states. Until such time as there is a case with national implications, the idea of right to privacy still hangs in the balance.

The Supreme Court sits at the apex of the American federal court system. The other two major components of the federal court system are the federal courts of appeal and the federal district courts. There are thirteen courts of appeals in the system. They are responsible for reviewing lower court decisions and the decisions of adjudicating federal agencies such as the Securities and Exchange Commission and the Federal Election Commission. There are ninety four federal district courts in the federal system. The federal district courts are courts of original jurisdiction. Original jurisdiction refers to the fact that federal cases are first heard in the district courts.

THE PHILOSOPHICAL STATUS OF THE SUPREME COURT

The Supreme Court is not only the highest court in the United States, its rulings become the highest legal dispensation in the nation. Such a position transcends religious beliefs, ideological world views, or the question of objective, immutable, and eternal truth. This power includes issues of life and death. For example, the Eighth Amendment prohibits "cruel and unusual punishment." Opponents of the death penalty argue that the ability of the state to put someone to death should be ruled unconstitutional. At one point in the American political narrative, the death penalty was declared unconstitutional in Furman v. Georgia 1972. But just three years later, the Court reversed itself on the death penalty in Gregg v. Georgia.[1] This raises the question, "What is the objective truth about the state putting someone to death?" At one point in the American political narrative the Supreme Court stated that "separate but equal" was constitutional. This 1896 Plessy v. Ferguson ruling paved the way for Jim Crow segregation and racial inequality throughout the United States. The landmark Brown v. Board of Education case in 1954 reversed Plessy by stating that "separate but equal" is unconstitutional. This ruling formed the basis of the civil rights movement, which lasted until 1968. Ironically, the civil rights movement and the Warren Court parallel one another.

As a consequence of the Supreme Court's position vis-à-vis objective truth, a major question is raised regarding the implementation of law. Dr. King addressed the question of just and unjust law in 1963 in his "Letter from Birmingham Jail:"

> *You express a great deal of anxiety over our willingness to break laws. This is certainly a legitimate concern. Since we so diligently urge people to obey the Supreme Court's decision of 1954 outlawing segregation in the public schools, it is rather strange and paradoxical to find us consciously breaking laws. One may well ask: "How can you advocate breaking some laws and obeying others?" The answer is found in the fact that there are two types of laws: There are just laws and there are unjust laws. I would be the first to advocate obeying just laws. One has not only a legal but moral responsibility to obey just laws. Conversely, one has a moral responsibility to disobey unjust laws. I would agree with Saint Augustine that "An unjust law is no law at all."*
>
> *Now what is the difference between the two? How does one determine when a law is just or unjust? A just law is a man-made code that squares with the moral law or the law of God.*

1 http://www.casebriefs.com/blog/law/criminal-law/criminal-law-keyed-to-kadish/homicide/gregg-v-georgia-2/

An unjust law is a code that is out of harmony with the moral law. To put it in the terms of Saint Thomas Aquinas, an unjust law is a human law that is not rooted in eternal and natural law. Any law that uplifts human personality is just. Any law that degrades human personality is unjust. All segregation statutes are unjust because segregation distorts the soul and damages the personality. It gives the segregator a false sense of superiority and the segregated a false sense of inferiority. To use the words of Martin Buber, the great Jewish philosopher, segregation substitutes an "I-it" relationship for an "I-thou" relationship, and ends up relegating persons to the status of things. So segregation is not only politically, economically, and sociologically unsound, but it is morally wrong and sinful. Paul Tillich has said that sin is separation. Isn't segregation an existential expression of man's tragic separation, an expression of his awful estrangement, his terrible sinfulness? So I can urge men to obey the1954 decision of the Supreme Court because it is morally right, and I can urge them to disobey segregation ordinances because they are morally wrong.

Let us turn to a more concrete example of just and unjust laws. An unjust law is a code that a majority inflicts on a minority that is not binding on itself. This is difference made legal. On the other hand a just law is a code that a majority compels a minority to follow that it is willing to follow itself. This is sameness made legal.

Let me give another explanation. An unjust law is a code inflicted upon a minority which that minority had no part in enacting or creating because they did not have the unhampered right to vote. Who can say that the legislature of Alabama which set up the segregation laws was democratically elected? Throughout the state of Alabama all types of conniving methods are used to prevent Negroes from becoming registered voters and there are some counties without a single Negro registered to vote despite the fact that the Negro constitutes a majority of the population. Can any law set up in such a state be considered democratically structured?

These are just a few examples of unjust and just laws. There are some instances when a law is just on its face but unjust in its application. For instance, I was arrested Friday on a charge of parading without a permit. Now there is nothing wrong with an ordinance which requires a permit for a parade, but when the ordinance is used to preserve segregation and to deny citizens the First Amendment privilege of peaceful assembly and peaceful protest, then it becomes unjust.

I hope you can see the distinction I am trying to point out. In no sense do I advocate evading or defying the law as the rabid segregationist would do. This would lead to anarchy. One who breaks an unjust law must do it openly, lovingly (not hatefully as the white mothers did in New Orleans when they were seen on television screaming "nigger, nigger, nigger") and with a willingness to accept the penalty. I submit that an individual who breaks a law that conscience tells him is unjust, and willingly accepts the penalty by staying in jail to arouse the conscience of the community over its injustice, is in reality expressing the very highest respect for law.

Of course there is nothing new about this kind of civil disobedience. It was seen sublimely in the refusal of Shadrach, Meshach, and Abednego to obey the laws of Nebuchadnezzar because a higher moral law was involved. It was practiced superbly by the early Christians who were willing to face hungry lions and the excruciating pain of chopping blocks, before submitting to certain unjust laws of the Roman Empire. To a degree academic freedom is a reality today because Socrates practiced civil disobedience.

We can never forget that everything Hitler did in Germany was "legal" and everything the Hungarian freedom fighters did in Hungary was "illegal." It was "illegal" to aid and comfort a

Jew in Hitler's Germany. But I am sure that, if I had lived in Germany during that time, I would have aided and comforted my Jewish brothers even though it was illegal. If I lived in a communist country today where certain principles dear to the Christian faith are suppressed, I believe I would openly advocate disobeying these anti-religious laws.[2]

Contemporary general consensus leads us to agree with Dr. King. Yet, the issue of squaring national law with the law of God can be problematic. Upon which religion should the secular square? Is Roe v. Wade 1973 in harmony with the laws of God? Are states that attempt to constrict or deny a woman the right to choose more in line with universal law? Would Dr. King be in agreement with the Court's current propensity to allow the limiting of voting rights?

According to the Constitution, Supreme Court justices are given lifetime appointments. The purpose of this arrangement was to place the Court above the fray of politics. Nevertheless, the political insulation of the Court from politics has not stopped presidents, who are intensely political, from attempting to fashion a Court in their own image. The most egregious attempt to fashion the Court was the court packing scheme put forth by Franklin Roosevelt. Irritated by the Court's invalidation of many pieces of his New Deal legislation, Roosevelt proposed the Judicial Procedures Reform Bill of 1937. The bill proposed that for every justice seventy and older, the president would be permitted to nominate an additional Justice. This scheme could have expanded the Court to fifteen justices. The plan was abandoned after it proved politically infeasible. Ever since Federalist Chief Justice John Marshall preserved the Federalist legacy, it has been understood that a president or party's legacy can be preserved long after that president or party is no longer in power. The Roberts Court's conservative majority is a legacy of three Republican presidents (Ronald Reagan, George H. W. Bush, and George W. Bush. Aside from electing presidents of the United States, the Supreme Court's legacy gives added importance to each presidential election.

2 Martin Luther King, Jr., "Letter from Birmingham Jail." Copyright in the Public Domain. (http://www.loveallpeople.org/letterfromthebirminghamcityjail.html)

5 CIVIL LIBERTIES

Civil liberties in the United States came as a major compromise during the writing of the Constitution in the summer of 1787. The debate concerning limits on government happened between the Federalists and Anti-Federalists. The Federalists favored a strong central government. The Anti-Federalists placed more emphasis on limiting the power of the central government for fear that, after casting off the tyranny of monarchy, a new tyranny could arise. Federalists, on the other hand, were compelled by the failure of the Articles of Confederation due to the fact that the states wielded most of the power and authority under the Articles of Confederation. Such a constitutional arrangement would make it difficult for a government to survive. Determined not to repeat the mistakes of the Articles, the framers of the Constitution pushed for more power for the central government. The Anti-Federalists, on the other hand, were leery of central authority or the concentration of power. Anti-Federalists wanted more safeguards against the government than what the Federalists argued were already present in the pre-Amendment Constitution. According to Federalists, safeguards to protect liberty were already present as evidenced by the following:

Article I, Section 9, Paragraph 2: The privilege of the Writ of Habeas Corpus shall not be suspended, unless when in Cases of Rebellion or Invasion the public Safety may require it.

Article I, Section 9, Paragraph 3: No Bill of Attainder or ex post facto Law shall be passed.[1]

The Writ of Habeas Corpus is "employed to bring a person before a court, most frequently to ensure the party's imprisonment or detention is not illegal" (Black's Law Dictionary, 8th ed). A Bill of Attainder "is a special legislative act prescribing punishment, without a trial, for a specific person or group (Black's Law Dictionary, 8th ed). An ex post facto law is applied retroactively in order to criminalize behavior after it has been performed. Based on these aspects of the pre-amended Constitution and safeguards against burdensome taxation, Federalists believed that enough protections were already a part of the Constitution and a Bill of Rights was not needed. The Bill of Rights was the product of an essential compromise that had to occur in order for the new government to come into existence.

TABLE 5.1

First Amendment:	Freedom of speech, religion, the press, and freedom to Petition the Government, and to Assemble.
Second Amendment:	The right to bear arms.
Third Amendment:	Quartering of troops.
Fourth Amendment:	The people are secure in their papers; prohibition against unreasonable searches and seizures.
Fifth Amendment:	Property rights, due process of law protecting property rights, freedom from self-incrimination.
Sixth Amendment:	Right to counsel.
Seventh Amendment:	Right to trial by jury.
Eight Amendment:	Cruel and unusual punishment.
Ninth Amendment:	Power reserved to the people (right to privacy).
Tenth Amendment:	Power of the states.

1 Copyright in the Public Domain.

The Bill of Rights was ratified in 1791. Nevertheless, there was an essential loophole in the Anti-Federalists argument against strong central government. States themselves could exercise tyrannical government. With the focus on limiting national government, the states were overlooked. This was revealed in the 1833 case of Barron v. Baltimore. There was no mechanism in the Constitution that could tie the Bill of Rights to the states. This remained true until the passage of the second Civil War Amendment in 1868 also known as the Fourteenth Amendment. Nevertheless, it was not until 1925 that the Supreme Court expressly stated that the Bill of Rights does apply to the states. The case was Gitlow v. New York. It involved the state of New York's 1917 Espionage Act. The law was allowed to stand, but in the Court's opinion it was stated that the Bill of Rights applies to the states by way of the Fourteenth Amendment. No one ruling, however, has tied the Bill of Rights to the states. The process of tying the Bill of Rights to the states is known as the incorporation doctrine.

The narrative of Constitutional Law is essentially the narrative of linking the Bill of Rights to the states. Freedom of speech cases include Gitlow v. New York 1925 and Schenck v. United States 1919. In a curious twist even campaign finance has come under the rubric of speech. Money first became equated with free speech in the case Buckley v. Valeo 1976. Subsequent to this case, Citizens United v. FEC was credited with opening the door to unlimited spending on behalf of political campaigns based on money being given free speech protection. Religion has also known a tumultuous effort at incorporation. The freedom of religion has two different aspects. First, there is the establishment clause, which prohibits the establishment of an official religion. Engle v. Vitale, for example, found school prayer to be unconstitutional. Abington v. Schempp declared Bible reading in public schools to be unconstitutional. Second there is the free exercise clause. Aside from the prohibition of the establishment of an official religion, people are allowed to practice their respective religions.

There have been movements to amend the constitution in order to provide for school prayer and bible readings. These sentiments are mostly expressed by the Religious Right or evangelicals in the United States. When George W. Bush became president, he issued an executive order establishing faith-based initiatives. President Barack Obama did not abolish faith-based initiatives; he only amended them with an executive order entitled Faith Based and Community Partnership.

The Second Amendment has been one of the more unsettled amendments for those who try to discern what the writers of the Constitution intended. It has been argued that, given the context of maintaining a well-regulated militia, the reference to the "people" in the Second Amendment refers to the states rather than individuals. The argument that the Second Amendment refers to individuals has only been adopted by the Supreme Court recently. The adoption of this language occurred in two essential cases involving Washington, D.C. and Chicago, Illinois. The D.C. case was the District of Columbia v. Keller. The Chicago case was Chicago v. McDonald. In Keller, the Supreme Court ruled that the Second Amendment protected the individual right to bear arms. In McDonald, the Court expressly stated that states could not infringe upon the rights of citizens to bear arms. The increase in mass shootings and the escalating gun violence in the city of Chicago has called into question the proliferation of guns in the United States. After the Sandy Hook school shooting, President Obama issued executive orders regarding gun regulation.

Cases involving the Fourth and Fifth Amendments have established very important doctrines related to limiting the power of the national government and, by way of the Fourteenth Amendment, the states. For example Mapp v. Ohio 1961 ruled against illegal searches. Guidelines have been established for securing evidence. Illegally obtained evidence is not admissible in a court of law. Miranda v. Arizona 1966 established the "Miranda Warning," which states that arrested suspects must be informed of their rights under the Fifth Amendment to the Constitution. The Fifth Amendment is also associated with the right from self-incrimination. Pleading the "Fifth" has become such a popular phrase that some fail to realize that this is one of the freedoms provided for in the Bill of Rights. The right to counsel under the Sixth Amendment was applied to the states by the case Gideon v. Wainwright 1963.

RIGHT TO PRIVACY

The Fifth Amendment also provides for the protection of property. Property cannot be confiscated by the government without "due process." It is implied by this provision that property includes private property. Nevertheless, the Constitution does not explicitly state that one has a right to privacy. The Constitution has been interpreted as including the concept of privacy. The essential Amendments that imply a right to privacy include the Third Amendment, Fourth Amendment, Fifth Amendment, and the Ninth Amendment. The implication for privacy in the Third Amendment is drawn from the clause that states, "no Soldier shall, in time of peace be quartered in any house without the consent of the Owner." The Fourth Amendment proclaims that "the right of the people to be secure in their persons, houses, papers, and effects, against unreasonable searches, and seizures, shall not be violated." The Fifth Amendment, as previously stated, says, "nor shall any person ... be deprived of life, liberty, or property, without due process of law; nor shall private property be taken for public use without just compensation." The bedrock amendment for a right to privacy is the Ninth Amendment, which reads "The enumeration in the Constitution of certain rights shall not be construed to deny or disparage others retained by the people." The first case to explicitly state that there is a right to privacy in the Constitution was Griswold v. Connecticut 1965. Roe v. Wade 1973, based the right of a woman to have an abortion on the Ninth Amendment. Other privacy cases include Loving v. Virginia 1967, Bowers v. Hardwick 1986, Lawrence v. Texas 2003, and a recent case involving same-sex marriage. The Supreme Court reversed itself in the Hardwick and Texas cases.

Capital punishment is another major topic of debate surrounding the Bill of Rights. The Eighth Amendment prohibits "cruel and unusual punishment." On its face, capital punishment seems inherently "cruel and unusual." Nevertheless, governments have executed members of their respective populations for centuries. The United States is no different. Yet, the clause in the Preamble to the Constitution, which reads, "in order to form a more perfect Union," has led many to question the use of the death penalty. This has resulted in an extended case narrative beginning with Furman v. Georgia 1972. In this particular case, the Supreme Court ruled that capital punishment violated the Eighth Amendment. Gregg v. Georgia 1976 reversed Furman and reinstated the death penalty. A significant challenge to the death penalty was mounted in 1987. Aside from the cruel and unusual argument against the death penalty, there is also an argument of its unequal application. This applies to its application on a state-by-state basis and its application when race is involved. This was the basis of McCleskey v. Kemp 1987. During oral arguments it was demonstrated that a black person killing a white person was more likely to get the death penalty than a white person killing a black person. The Court ruled that although the statistics demonstrated that there was a racial disparity in the application of the death penalty, it did not meet the standard on which could constitute cruel and unusual punishment.

Arguments against the death penalty state that death, by its very nature involves cruelty. Others state that the death penalty is unevenly applied across states, with some states using the death penalty and other states prohibiting the death penalty:

1. Penry v. Lynaugh 1989
2. Stanford v. Kentucky 1989 (execution above age sixteen)
3. McCleskey v. Zant 1991
4. Keeney v. Tamayo-Reyes 1992
5. Atkins v. Virginia 2002 (cannot execute mentally challenged persons)
6. Roper v. Simmons 2005 (cannot be executed for crimes committed before age of eighteen)
7. Baze v. Rees 2008 (lethal injection)

The Supreme Court and Legal Dispensation

The Supreme Court decides many types of cases with myriad ramifications. Oftentimes cases can conflict with prevailing historical and contemporary values. Aside from being a nation of laws, America is also a very religious nation. It is debatable what the framers intended by "separation of church and state." Some argue that it placed America on the side of atheists. Others argue that it was simply intended to make sure that no one religion dominated or was given state sanction. There is a more poignant question that is raised by this particular arrangement and development. Religions profess to a God, a Higher Power, and Truth. This refers to truth in the uppercase sense, the ultimate, irrefutable, immutable Truth. In his "Letter from Birmingham Jail," Dr. King addressed the topic of just and unjust laws. Among his several points for distinguishing just laws from unjust laws, Dr. King said that a just law is one that squares with the laws of God. On the face of it, this sounds progressive. Such utterances coming from Dr. King are progressive. On the other hand, one can hear the very parishioners and ministers saying exactly the same thing in regards to segregation. Segregation, according to them, is ordained by God and flows from the natural order of things in a universe that was created by an all-knowing God. Such diverse perspectives leave one with an essential question. What is Truth? What is the ultimate, irrefutable, immutable Truth? For example, in Plessy v. Ferguson 1896 the Supreme Court ruled that separate but equal is constitutional. In 1954, the Supreme Court reversed itself and stated that separate but equal is unconstitutional. Is there an ultimate Truth in this debate? Perhaps one has a preferred Truth, but that does not determine the ultimate Truth. If one cannot discern the ultimate Truth, the only conclusion that is left is that the Supreme Court is the highest dispensation in the United States. Moral conflicts aside, there is no higher dispensation on a topic than the Supreme Court's ruling. More often than not these rulings are handed down by five justices. Other examples include rulings on sodomy laws. In 1986 in Bowers v. Hardwick, the Court ruled that sodomy laws are constitutional and in line with community standards or values. In 2003 the Supreme Court ruled that sodomy laws violated the right to privacy and, therefore, were not constitutional.

The issue of highest dispensation becomes extremely critical in assessing the course of a nation. If there is no ultimate truth, the course of a nation is left to sheer political will. Prior to the passage of the Civil Rights Act of 1964 and the Voting Rights Act of 1965, Dr. King stated that the "arch of the universe is long, but it bends toward justice." The Civil Rights Act of 1964, which was essentially a reiteration of the Civil Rights Act of 1875, was found to be constitutional in the Heart of Atlanta Motel case. The 1875 law was deemed unconstitutional. Near the end of the Court's 2012–2013 term, the preclearance section of the Voting Rights Act of 1965 was found to be unconstitutional in the case Shelby County v. Holder 2013.

6 CIVIL RIGHTS AND SOCIAL MOVEMENTS

Thomas Jefferson, in the Declaration of Independence, stated, "We hold these truths to be self-evident that all men are created equal." Two of the more famous quotes and paraphrases of this declaration include the Declaration of Sentiments in 1848 and Dr. Martin Luther King's "I Have a Dream Speech" in 1963. Both quotes focus on the issue of equality. However, equality did not become a major ideal for America until the Fourteenth Amendment to the Constitution. Prior to the Fourteenth Amendment, equality was raised as an issue as it pertained to the states. The Connecticut Compromise called for equal representation in order to afford the smaller states an equal footing with the larger states during the writing of the Constitution. The Tenth Amendment to the Constitution also assures that the states are given constitutional sanction in the governing of the United States. Jefferson's declaration of equality was a principle concerning individuals that was not given legal sanction until the Fourteenth Amendment's equal protection clause. Even more than this, it is a question as to whom Jefferson had in mind when he composed such lofty ideals.

Equality before the law establishes the basis for civil rights. The Thirteenth Amendment to the Constitution ended constitutionally sanctioned chattel enslavement of Black people in the United States. Nevertheless, there was an "except clause" that formed a loophole that transformed enslavement to an aspect of the penal system. This was evident in the immediate aftermath of the Civil War when various laws and ordinances were passed by state and local governments in order to target the black population for mass incarceration. Aside from equal protection under the laws, the Fourteenth Amendment provided the formerly enslaved with citizenship rights. The Fifteenth Amendment extended the franchise to Black male citizens. With those amendments, the idea of equality became firmly implanted within the American constitutional fabric. Although the Civil War amendments provided a basis for equality, equality before the law proved a major struggle for years to come. Prior to the Civil War there were two essential movements that attempted to move the nation more in line with the idea of equality and freedom based on more than property: the Abolition Movement and the Suffrage Movement, which both proved successful given eventual changes to the Constitution.

President Truman issued Executive Order 9981 in 1948 desegregating the military. Although racial discrimination did not cease immediately, Truman's order paved the way for a more integrated military and the possibility of advancement for troops of color. Issues regarding discrimination against Blacks in the United States arose during the presidency of Franklin Roosevelt. Union activists A. Philip Randolph and Bayard Rustin had lobbied Roosevelt for fair employment practices in the defense industry. Their essential leverage was the call for a march on Washington. The groundwork for such a call was conducted by The March on Washington Movement. In an effort to head off the march, Roosevelt issued an Executive Order calling for fair hiring practices in those companies who contracted with the government for the purpose of defense. The March on Washington Movement was the precursor to the Civil Rights Movement.

THE CIVIL RIGHTS MOVEMENT AND CIVIL RIGHTS

The Civil Rights Movement can be dated from 1954 to 1968. It began with the Supreme Court decision in Brown v. Board of Education, which declared "separate but equal" to be unconstitutional. The Brown decision reversed Plessy v. Ferguson 1896, which established the legal dispensation of "separate but equal" as constitutional. The Plessy case involved interstate train travel, yet gave national sanction to Jim Crow and American apartheid in the United States. The Brown decision dealt with the issue of school desegregation. Nevertheless, it gave national legitimacy to Black aspirations for equal treatment under the law. The Brown decision was another example of a case in which the Supreme Court changed legal dispensations as it relates to governance in the United States. What had changed between Blacks and Whites between 1896 and 1954?

Had there been any biological changes? Had there been any new revelations from a higher power? The essential answer is that the Court changed its mind. Yet, one is left, once again, with the question regarding what the ultimate truth is in this situation. If there is not an ultimate truth, who is to say that another Court, at some point in the future, will not reverse Brown or narrow its understanding?

Shortly after the Brown decision, Rosa Parks was arrested in Birmingham, Alabama for refusing to relinquish her seat to a white patron on the bus. Many myths surround this particular incident. The "Old Negro Spiritual" myth states that Ms. Parks was tired after working hard all day. Her being tired was symbolic of Blacks in America being tired of second class treatment in the United States. The "Leadership Myth" is that Rosa Parks intentionally created this situation in order to draw attention to the segregation that continued even in the wake of the Brown v. Board decision. It is true that Rosa Parks was a member of the local NAACP and had been trained in protest methods. On the other hand, she is not the first person to have been arrested for not relinquishing her seat. There was another young woman who had been arrested a week earlier. It is difficult to determine what will trigger a movement of sustained resistance.

Major groups involved in the Civil Rights Movement include The National Association for the Advancement of Colored People (NAACP), the Urban League, the Student Nonviolent Coordinating Committee (SNCC), and the Southern Christian Leadership Council (SCLC). Martin Luther King, Jr. was the founder and first president of SCLC. The NAACP is the oldest civil rights organization. All of these groups shared the same goal but had different methods for achieving their goal. The principal goal was "universal freedom" for Black people in the United States.

The NAACP sought to bring about change through the Courts. The NAACP was created in 1909 in upstate New York as part of what was known as the Niagara Movement. The organization has achieved monumental success in the Courts regarding the Civil Right Movement. In 1944, the NAACP was successful in the Smith vs. Allwright case. This case found that the all White primary was unconstitutional. The southern part of the United States was considered a one party region dominated by the Democratic Party. Any candidate who won in a primary election was considered to have automatically won in the general election. Therefore, to exclude Blacks from the primary effectively eroded their votes. The most celebrated case fought by the NAACP is Brown v. Board of Education. Thurgood Marshall, who later was appointed to the Supreme Court, was a lead attorney on this case. In Brown, the Supreme Court ruled that "separate but equal" was unconstitutional. This reversed Plessy v. Ferguson, which had supplied the legal foundation for Jim Crow based on the principle that separate but equal was constitutional. The Brown Case focused on education. The Plessy Case centered on public transportation on the train.

The Brown v. Board of Education ruling predated the Montgomery Bus Boycott by just over a year. The successful culmination of the bus boycott led to the creation of the Southern Christian Leadership Conference (SCLC) in 1957. SCLC was an organizational embodiment of the philosophy of civil disobedience and non-violent direct action as advocated by Dr. King. Civil disobedience, as practiced by King was directly influenced by Henry David Thoreau and Mahatma Gandhi of India. Gandhi spoke of the soul force or Satyagraha. The main tenet of civil disobedience is that protesters who break the established laws in order to draw attention to injustice must be willing to face the consequences of their actions. Aside from the March on Washington, which was greatest moment of the Civil Rights Movement, SCLC also promoted sit-ins and freedom rides. Youth were a very important part of the civil rights coalition. Dr. King was criticized when he allowed school aged youth to participate in the Birmingham campaign. Nevertheless, students rose to the forefront of the movement. The

Student Nonviolent Coordinating Committee (SNCC) was created to capture the student energy of the movement. SNCC placed most of its emphasis on voter registration. Notable leaders of SNCC, included John Lewis, Eleanor Holmes Norton, and Stokely Carmichael. John Lewis spoke at the 1963 March on Washington. He was badly beaten during the first attempt to stage a march across the Edmund Pettus Bridge in Selma, Alabama, in order to dramatize the need to protect voting rights. John Lewis currently serves as a member of the House of Representatives from a district that covers Atlanta, Georgia. Eleanor Holmes Norton also serves in Congress as non-voting member representing the District of Columbia. Stokely Carmichael would later change his name to Kwame Ture and form an organization called the All African Peoples Revolutionary Party (AAPRP). Before becoming a leader of SNCC, he was credited with popularizing the phrase "Black Power." The Black Power Movement would eventually challenge Dr. King's non-violent movement with what Dr. King referred to as the "marvelous new militancy."

The Urban League was less confrontational than any of the aforementioned organizations. The Urban League placed a great deal of emphasis on prepping people of color to participate within the corporate sphere. Although the Urban League was less confrontational, its members still participated in the Civil Rights Movement. A signature contribution of the Urban League today is its annual publication *The State of Black America.* Each year this publication publishes a number of indicators assessing the progress of Blacks in American society.

Writings about the Civil Rights Movement are often confusing. Groups that were not a part of the Civil Rights Movement are often cavalierly listed as civil rights leaders or civil right organizations. For example, the Black Panther Party for Self Defense was not a civil rights organization. Created in 1966 in Oakland, California, the Black Panther Party was created as a reaction to police violence. They created breakfast programs to feed school-aged children and advocated their rights to own weapons under the Second Amendment to the Constitution. The Black Panther Party was at one time called the greatest threat to America by FBI Director J. Edgar Hoover. Based on this belief, Hoover set about trying to destroy the Black Panther Party. The FBI also attempted to discredit King. The umbrella under which Hoover attempted to derail these organizations was known as COINTELPRO or Counter Intelligence Program.

Other individuals and organizations mischaracterized under the civil rights movement included Malcolm X, the Nation of Islam, and US. US is an organization created by Maulana Karenga. Karenga created the Kwanzaa Holiday. It should be noted that Malcolm X was not a civil rights leader. Malcolm X was a spokesperson for the Nation of Islam, which was led by the Honorable Elijah Mohammed. Malcolm X was assassinated in 1965 after leaving the Nation of Islam to start his own organization. Malcolm X focused more on human rights issues that transcended any government.

THE ABOLITION OF AFRICAN ENSLAVEMENT

The issue of abolition existed in order to bring about an end to African enslavement in the United States. One of the major leaders in the Abolition Movement was Frederick Douglass. Douglass had been formally enslaved himself. William Lloyd Garrison was also instrumental in the Abolition Movement. Some of the outcomes of the movement included the creation of the African country of Liberia. Many formerly enslaved Africans were repatriated to the continent as Liberians. The capital of the country was named after President James Monroe.

VOTING RIGHTS

Prominent names that emerged from the Suffrage Movement included Susan B. Anthony and Elizabeth Cady Stanton. A major marker for the Suffrage Movement was the Seneca Falls Convention, which was held in Seneca Falls, New York. The essential document that emerged from the convention was The Declaration of Sentiments.

The Suffrage Movement achieved its greatest success with the ratification of the Nineteenth Amendment. The Nineteenth Amendment reads as follows: "The right of citizens of the United States to vote shall not be denied or abridged by the United States or by any State on account of sex."

The drive to achieve voting rights for women was accompanied by a push for other rights articulated by the Declaration of Sentiments For example, the Equal Rights Amendment was proposed in 1923. Although it was proposed in 1923, it did not pass Congress until 1972. It was given a ten-year period for ratification. Debates over the amendment were divided and quite pointed. In the final analysis, the amendment failed at ratification. It failed to gain support from three-fourths of the states, which is the constitutional threshold for amendments to the Constitution.

America's particular story of voting begins with a majority of Black people confined to "involuntary servitude." Blacks were existing in America with no constitutional protections until the ratification of the Thirteenth Amendment in 1865 and the Fourteenth Amendment in 1868. It should be noted that the ratification battle over the Thirteenth Amendment served as the narrative for the hit movie *Lincoln*. The year 1870 saw the ratification of the Fifteenth Amendment to the Constitution. This amendment stated that voting could not be abridged due to one's race. The immediate effect of the amendment was to expand the franchise to Black men. Congress, in the same year, experienced its first senators and congressmen of African descent. Irrespective of this advance, both Black women and White women were still denied the right to vote in the United States. Nevertheless, the ratification of the Fifteenth Amendment marked the beginning of an expansion of voting rights that consequently translated into an expansion of democracy. The Fifteenth Amendment along with the Thirteenth and Fourteenth Amendments are known as the Civil War Amendments. Aside from coming on the heels of the Civil War, these amendments were an outgrowth of the Abolitionist Movement, which ran parallel to the Women's Suffrage Movement. Women did not receive the right to vote until the Nineteenth Amendment was ratified in 1920. Ironically, some argue that this first/second reality was repeated in 2008 when a Black male became president before a woman did.

Expansion of the franchise began to reverse after the presidential election of 1876, due to the end of Reconstruction. Expansion slowed even further with the 1896 Supreme Court decision in Plessy v. Ferguson, which gave America the political and legal dispensation of "separate but equal." In short, 1896 saw the acceleration of voting rights contraction. Black voting, in particular, was targeted for elimination or suppression. History is littered with such terms as "literacy test," "grandfather clause," and "poll tax." All these terms are associated with the targeted contraction of Black voting rights. Although the Supreme Court found poll taxes unconstitutional in 1964, this prolonged contraction culminated in the "Bloody Sunday March." Marchers for voting rights were met with stiff and brutal resistance from Alabama state police as they attempted to cross the Edmund Pettus Bridge on their way to Montgomery, Alabama. Events surrounding this march serve as the backdrop for the hit movie *Selma*. On August 6, 1965 President Lyndon Johnson signed the Voting Rights Act into law. The Voting Rights Act linked the Fourteenth and Nineteenth Amendments in order to secure the voting rights of both Black men and Black women. Once again voting rights for African Americans began to expand. On the heels of the new law Shirley Chisholm became the first Black woman elected to Congress. Subsequently, Barbara Jordan became the first Black Woman elected to Congress from the south post Reconstruction. The Congressional Black Caucus was created, and the number of Blacks serving in Congress began to grow with the ensuing decades.

This expansion was complemented by other presidents, both Democrats and Republicans. The Twenty-Sixth Amendment expanded the franchise to eighteen-year-olds in 1971. The Motor Voter Act of 1993 was enacted in order to facilitate voter registration and expand the franchise even further. Ronald Reagan agreed, reluctantly, to extend the Voting Rights Act. George W. Bush also agreed to extend the Voting Rights Act. Although there were rumblings of discontent from covered jurisdictions and the extreme right, a consensus of both Democrats and Republicans believed that the country had a compelling interest in preserving African American voting rights. Ironically, this consensus on African American voting rights all changed in 2008 with the election of the first Black president.

LESBIAN, GAY, BISEXUAL, AND TRANSEXUAL (LGBT) RIGHTS

President Obama linked gay issues, women's issues, and civil rights issues together in his second inaugural address. The Stonewall Rebellion is seen as a landmark event in the gay movement. The 1969 Stonewall Rebellion marked a series of protests on the part of gay activists that was precipitated by a New York City police raid on the Stonewall Inn. The Stonewall Inn had become a safe haven for gay individuals to gather in New York City. Key rights that gay Americans have fought for include acceptance in the military, same-sex marriage, and hate crime legislation. Violence against gays has been a specter in American society. One of the more sensational cases involved Matthew Shepherd who was beaten to death. A series of cases and laws have come to shape the debate related to same-sex marriage. In 1996, Congress passed and President Clinton signed into law the Defense of Marriage Act, which defined marriage in the United States as the union between one man and one woman. The legislation was passed in order to head off efforts by states to legalize same-sex marriage.

NOTES

Branch, Taylor. *Parting the Waters: America in the King Years 1954–1963.* New York: Simon & Schuster, 1988.

Branch, Taylor. *Pillar of Fire: America in the King Years 1963–1965.* New York: Simon & Schuster, 1998.

7 INTEREST GROUPS

James Madison, in Federalist #10, warned of the undue influence of factions. The First Amendment to the Constitution offers protection for various rights and freedoms in the United States. One such right protected by the First Amendment is the "right of the people ... to petition the Government for a redress of grievances." This right has mostly been carried out by citizens coalescing around a shared interest and lobbying the government. Such groups of citizens are known as interest groups. Interest groups in the United States appear and function in very diverse ways. The vast majority fall into either one of two categories. There are both private and public interest groups. Private interest groups tend to represent major economic interests of the business sector consisting of several industries. One need only to take a brief look through the most recent issue of the *Fortune 500* or *Forbes 400* to identify many major economic interests in the United States. Some of the leading industries include automobiles, telecommunications, agriculture, the National Football League (NFL), the National Basketball Association (NBA), pharmaceuticals, retailers, home builders, banks, social media, airline, retailers, engineering, and construction. Wealthy individuals range from billionaire sports franchise owners to major corporate executives.

Private interest groups seek to maximize their interests by lobbying members of Congress, members of the executive branch of government, and state governors and legislators. Legislatures pass the laws while the executive branch of government functions to see that the "laws are faithfully executed." Private interest groups play what is known as the "inside game" of politics. The inside game of politics seeks to change laws and regulations or defend the status quo by having a cozy relationship with lawmakers, executives, and bureaucrats. According to the inside game, it is important to maintain a relationship with lawmakers in order to secure laws that are favorable to one's interests. A strong metaphor for analyzing the inside game is the Iron Triangle. The very definition of the Iron Triangle is a cozy relationship between private interests, Congress, and the Executive Branch of government. The Iron Triangle can be further refined to incorporate congressional committees and executive agencies along with private interests. Once again private interests entail various industries such as oil, entertainment, sports, automobile, coal, home builders, retailers, telecommunications, insurance, and wealthy individuals. Congress is defined by individual senators and members of the House of Representatives as well as committees, subcommittees, and staffers. Moreover, as stated, the work of Congress is performed within committees. The Executive branch is defined by Cabinet-level departments, agencies, bureaus, and commissions. It is also important to maintain a relationship with bureaucrats due to the fact that bureaucrats implement law enforcement regulations. Various agencies such as the Securities and Exchange Commission and the Federal Communications Commission also issue rules and adjudicate numerous issues that arise long after the passage of legislation. An important publication to watch in this regard is the *Federal Register*. The government publishes proposed new rules and rule changes in the *Federal Register*. Private interests usually monitor the *Federal Register* in order to address proposed rule changes in the applications of legislation/laws passed by Congress. This activity fits within the constitutional mandate of the executive branch to "see that the laws are faithfully executed." There are two major pieces of legislation that illustrate the role of Congress, private interests, and the executive branch as they pertain to the Iron Triangle. The first example relates to the Telecommunications Act of 1996. The Affordable Care Act of 2010 provides our second example.

***The Telecommunications Act of 1996*:** The stated purpose of the Telecommunications Act of 1996 was to ensure more competition in the area of telecommunications. For example, under the act, companies such as Verizon now are able to offer various services such as television in addition to land-line and wireless phone service.

***The Affordable Healthcare Act of 2010*:** The Affordable Healthcare Act of 2010 was a signature piece of legislation of the Obama administration. Since its passage, millions more Americans have been able to secure health insurance. Supporters of expanded health care advocated for a single-payer system with the government at the center much like Social Security and Medicare. Free market backers preferred private insurance companies to become providers instead of the federal government. In the final analysis, the private insurance companies won out on the strength of their lobbying efforts.

There are two essential ways in which to view interest groups. The first is through the Iron Triangle. The second way is through pluralism. Pluralism is the belief that all groups in American society will have the opportunity to influence government at some point. Pluralism holds that individual citizens, aside from voting, find meaningful participation in the political system through membership in interest groups. (This view of interest groups would find more participation in public interest groups.) These interest groups place more emphasis on promoting the public good. Such groups can also be found in the area of civil rights. For example, one might argue that African Americans constitute a group or segment of society. However, it is through interest groups that their particular interests are promoted. A long list of African American interest groups have participated in the advancement of civil rights in general and the advancement of people of color in particular. These groups include: the National Association for the Advancement of Colored People (NAACP), Southern Christian Leadership Council (SCLC), Student Nonviolent Coordination Committee (SNCC), the Urban League, and Operation PUSH (People United to Save Humanity). The NAACP is the oldest of these civil rights organizations. It was founded in 1909. The court system was the principal method for change used by the NAACP. Brown v. Board of Education is one the organization's signature victories. The Urban League has placed a great deal of emphasis on bringing opportunity through business and corporate sponsorship. As stated, many of these interest groups used outsider tactics to bring about change.

8 POLITICAL PARTIES

Political parties are organizations that often run candidates for political offices with the goal of running the government. They are often conduits for ideological perspectives regarding social policy and governance. Unlike social movements that seek to influence government from the outside or interest groups that primarily seek to influence government through information and inside contacts, political parties seek to influence government by controlling the reins of power. Political parties were not present at the creation of the United States. There were, however, very strong opinions on what shape the new nation should take as it pertains to the type government that should be instituted. These very strong ideas began to crystallize in George Washington's first cabinet.

George Washington sought to rise above party by seeking compromise at home and neutrality abroad. Yet, he was often buffeted by two members of his cabinet who did not agree on very many issues. Thomas Jefferson was Washington's first Secretary of State. He was more inclined to favor the French and advocated for a small central government giving more power to the states. Alexander Hamilton was Washington's first Secretary of the Treasury and offered more support toward Great Britain. Jefferson's followers eventually coalesced into what became known as the Democratic Republicans or Jeffersonian Republicans. Hamilton's followers became known as the Federalists. When George Washington left office he was aware of the growing divisions in the country. In his farewell address to the nation, he cautioned the nation not to allow factions to come between themselves and their government. According to Washington:

> *Towards the preservation of your government, and the permanency of your present happy state, it is requisite, not only that you steadily discountenance irregular oppositions to its acknowledged authority, but also that you resist with care the spirit of innovation upon its principles, however specious the pretexts. One method of assault may be to effect, in the forms of the* Constitution, *alterations which will impair the energy of the system, and thus to undermine what cannot be directly overthrown. In all the changes to which you may be invited, remember that time and habit are at least as necessary to fix the true character of governments as of other human institutions; that experience is the surest standard by which to test the real tendency of the existing constitution of a country; that facility in changes, upon the credit of mere hypothesis and opinion, exposes to perpetual change, from the endless variety of hypothesis and opinion; and remember, especially, that for the efficient management of your common interests, in a country so extensive as ours, a government of as much vigor as is consistent with the perfect security of liberty is indispensable. Liberty itself will find in such a government, with powers properly distributed and adjusted, its surest guardian. It is, indeed, little else than a name, where the government is too feeble to withstand the enterprises of faction, to confine each member of the society within the limits prescribed by the laws, and to maintain all in the secure and tranquil enjoyment of the rights of person and property.*[1]

The first election that pitted Jefferson's party against Hamilton's party was the election of 1796. Although the parties had not totally crystallized, the ideological basis of the parties was quite evident.

1 George Washington, from George Washington's Farewell Address. Copyright in the Public Domain (1796).

Therefore, the election of 1796 saw the states' rights, Thomas Jefferson, and the strong central government John Adams as the principal candidates. Jefferson was the candidate for the Democratic Republicans. Adams represented the Federalist Party. John Adams had also served as vice president under George Washington. Given the constitutional structure of the election as set forth in Article II of the Constitution, Adams was elected as president. Thomas Jefferson was elected as vice president. Perhaps this would not have been a problem except for the development of political parties. Therefore, the election of 1796 resulted in a president and vice president from different political parties. This situation was soon rectified by the Twelfth Amendment to the Constitution. In contemporary presidential elections, the president and vice president form a clear single candidate ticket. John Adams served as a one-term president. He was the first and only Federalist party member to be elected president. Adams lost to Thomas Jefferson in the election of 1800.[2] This was a hard fought battle for party supremacy. In an effort to curb the fallout from the election, Thomas Jefferson addressed the divisions in his first Inaugural Address:

> *We are all Republicans, we are all Federalists. If there be any among us who would wish to dissolve this Union or to change its republican form, let them stand undisturbed as monuments of the safety with which error of opinion may be tolerated where reason is left free to combat it. I know, indeed, that some honest men fear that a republican government can not be strong, that this Government is not strong enough; but would the honest patriot, in the full tide of successful experiment, abandon a government which has so far kept us free and firm on the theoretic and visionary fear that this Government, the world's best hope, may by possibility want energy to preserve itself? I trust not. I believe this, on the contrary, the strongest Government on earth. I believe it the only one where every man, at the call of the law, would fly to the standard of the law, and would meet invasions of the public order as his own personal concern. Sometimes it is said*

2 Larson 2007.

that man can not be trusted with the government of himself. Can he, then, be trusted with the government of others? Or have we found angels in the forms of kings to govern him? Let history answer this question.[3]

Presidential candidate Barack Obama also addressed the issue of party division in his 2004 Keynote Address at the Democratic National Convention:

> *Yet even as we speak, there are those who are preparing to divide us, the spin masters and negative ad peddlers who embrace the politics of anything goes. Well, I say to them tonight, there's not a liberal America and a conservative America—there's the United States of America. There's not a black America and white America and Latino America and Asian America; there's the United States of America. The pundits like to slice-and-dice our country into Red States and Blue States; Red States for Republicans, Blue States for Democrats. But I've got news for them, too. We worship an awesome God in the Blue States, and we don't like federal agents poking around our libraries in the Red States. We coach Little League in the Blue States and have gay friends in the Red States. There are patriots who opposed the war in Iraq and patriots who supported it. We are one people, all of us pledging allegiance to the stars and stripes, all of us defending the United States of America.*[4]

THE ROLE OF POLITICAL PARTIES

1. Political parties secure candidates to run for political office.
2. Political parties embody ideals and ideas about governing.

---

3 Thomas Jefferson, from Thomas Jefferson's Inaugural Address. Copyright in the Public Domain (March 4, 1801).

4 Barack Obama, from Keynote Address at the Democratic National Convention. Copyright © 2004 by Barack Obama. (http://www.pbs.org/newshour/bb/politics-july-dec04-obama-keynote-dnc/)

3. Political parties provide accountability to the electorate.
4. Political parties seek to control government.
5. Political parties seek to maintain themselves through coalitions.

The essential reason for the existence of political parties is to offer a candidate for office in order to control the reins of government. Political parties function on all levels of government. This includes the national, state, and local levels. At the local level parties, seem to be more important at the county level than at the municipal level. Consequently, you have party organizations that mirror this reality. Both Democrats and Republicans have county, state, and national party organizations. At the national level, the office of president is the essential prize. Every four years the national party organization is in charge of the national nomination convention. This usually occurs after the primary and has come to be the coronation ceremony of what has already been determined during the primary process. At the state level the governorship becomes the primary focus. The state legislatures are also important based on which party dominates in the respective states.

Political parties incorporate the ideological basis of those who have coalesced around a particular party. With the dominance of Democrats and Republicans, this centers on conservative versus liberal perspectives. Republicans hold to conservative ideas while Democrats hold to liberal ideas. This shows up on the map with Republicans represented by the color red and Democrats with the color blue. This is what Barack Obama meant by Red States and Blue States. These conservative and liberal perspectives also mirror early party formations around strong central government or more power to the states. Democrats tend to advocate more government while Republicans advocate smaller central government with more power to the states. Nevertheless, even this can be flipped if it is applied to personal liberty or right to privacy issues. In this context, Republicans tend to advocate more government intervention while Democrats tend to promote more personal liberty or a right to privacy.

Political parties also provide accountability for policies that are successful or policies that fail. At the presidential level this can be realized in two different ways. First, a sitting president can be rewarded with a second term. On the other hand, if this is the sitting president's second and last term, the sitting president's party successor can be rewarded by being elected to the office of president. This is what happened for George H. W. Bush in the election of 1988. As President Reagan's vice president, Bush was able to use Reagan's popularity and relative success for an advantage in his campaign for the office of president. However, the Republicans were held accountable for the downturn in the economy near the end of President Bush's first term. Consequently, the Democrats were able to secure the White House with Bill Clinton as president.

Party control of government has led to the phenomenon of "divided government." Divided government occurs when one party controls the presidency and the other party controls Congress or one House of Congress. For example, during President Obama's first two years in office, the Democrats controlled both Houses of Congress and the office of president. Slippage in the president's approval helped to award Republicans control of the House of Representatives after the midterm elections of 2010. This led to a divided government and a severe slowdown in governing. ***Divided government*** is a party phenomenon that serves as an overlay to America's system of separation of powers and checks and balances. This system was meant to serve as a type of adversarial system that would be based on compromise in order to produce policies that had been thoroughly vetted by the separation of powers system. Divided government has led to the possibility of governmental paralysis based on the inability or unwillingness to compromise based on ideological differences.

Coalitions serve as the central makeup of political parties. It would be difficult for a major political party to exist in America's two party system with a limited coalition or constituent base. The coalitions may shift over time. However, the basic tendencies of the political parties remain unchanged. This shift in coalitions is known as realignment. One of the most significant party realignments occurred along racial and geographical lines. Since the election of 1860, Democrats and Republicans have faced off at the national level for the office of president. In the election of 1860, Democrats controlled the southern part of the country. Republicans were sheltered in the north and west. It was the Democratic Party that seceded from the Union on the issue of African enslavement. It was also the southern wing of the Democratic

Party that fought against integration and civil rights during the 1950s and 1960s. One hundred years after the election of 1860, the election of 1960 found the northern liberal Democrat candidate and eventual president John F. Kennedy as the successor to President Lincoln. Ironically, the Republican candidate that Kennedy defeated would reemerge in the election of 1968 in order to claim Republican victory. Sensing southern dissatisfaction with the national Democratic Party's lean toward desegregation and civil rights, Richard Nixon engineered a southern strategy that proved successful for Republicans. In the mid-1960s, the south was still heavily Democratic. By the time of the election of Barack Obama to the presidency, the South had become solidly Republican. As it pertains to race, during the beginning of the 1960s there was still a large number of African Americans who identified as Republicans. Once again, by the time of the election of Bill Clinton to the office of president, African Americans were giving the Democrats 95 percent or more of their support. This trend tends to dismiss the notion that African Americans voted for Barack Obama simply because he was Black. A White Democratic candidate in 2008 and 2012 would more than likely have garnered the same level of Black support based on loyalty to the Democratic Party.

THE PERSISTENCE OF THE TWO-PARTY SYSTEM

The United States maintains a two-party system. This is not to say that there are only two political parties in the United States, but it is to say that there tend to be only two viable contending parties for the control of Congress and electing a president. Despite the myriad parties that have existed and still exist in the United States, only the Federalists, Democratic Republicans, Whigs, Republicans, and Democrats have elected individuals to the presidency of the United States. Since the election of 1860, only Democrats and Republicans have faced off as viable options for the office of president as well as for control of Congress.

The Federalist Party elected only one president. This was John Adams in the election of 1796. John Adams had served as Washington's vice president. Adams's one term presidency can be attributed to his policies as well as the failing demographics of the Federalist Party itself. Adams's foreign policy alienated hawkish Federalists by not going to war with France. Yet, his administration signed the Alien and Sedition Acts, which essentially targeted French dissent in the United States. This alienated followers of Jefferson who favored the French. De Tocqueville mentioned the demise of the Federalists in his 1831 book, *Democracy in America*. According to de Tocqueville, the Federalists became narrow in their outlook and essentially faded due to the inability to add to their coalition base. De Tocqueville wrote:

> *The means by which the Federalist had maintained their position were artificial, and their resources were temporary; it was by the virtues or the talents of their leaders that they had risen to power. When the Republicans attained to that lofty station, their opponents were overwhelmed by utter defeat. An immense majority declared itself against the retiring party, and the Federalists found themselves in so small a minority that they at once despaired of their success. From that moment the Republican or Democratic party has proceeded from conquest to conquest, until it has acquired absolute supremacy in the country. The Federalists, perceiving that they were vanquished without resource, and isolated in the midst of the nation, fell into two divisions, of which one joined the victorious Republicans, and the other abandoned its rallying-point and its name. Many years have already elapsed since they ceased to exist as a party.*[5]

Despite the diversity of opinions and interests in the United States, the two parties persist for three essential reasons. According to Maurice Duverger, the two-party system persists due to **single-member districts, winner-take-all elections, and plurality elections**. These three

5 Alexis de Tocqueville, from *Democracy in America*, trans. Henry Reeve, p. 172. Copyright in the Public Domain (www.gutenberg.org).

components are known as Duverger's Law. A single-member district means that only one individual can represent a particular legislative district. This also occurs on the local, state, or national levels. For example, there are 435 legislative districts that make up the House of Representatives. Only one person can represent each district. A winner-take-all election means that there is no proportional representation. Even if a third party were to garner 30 percent of the vote, the party in question would not be rewarded with 30 percent of the seats. A plurality election mean that an individual in a three-way race does not have to win a 50 plus percent of the vote. In such an election, the candidate with the highest percentage wins. In some communities, runoff elections are required if a candidate does not secure a certain percentage of the vote. Nevertheless, the end result is one winner, and that candidate takes all.

Significant third parties have arisen from time to time to challenge the prevailing two-party system; however, the viability of these particular parties has been short-lived. For example, Theodore Roosevelt led the Progressive "Bull Moose" Party in the election of 1912. Although his party won more electoral votes than the Republican Party, he did not win the presidency. The Progressives soon disbanded. Ross Perot created the Reform Party. This party was popular through the presidential election cycles of 1988 and 1992. The greatest success that the Reform Party experienced was the election of Reform Party candidate Jesse Ventura as governor of Minnesota in 1998. Perennial presidential candidate and consumer activist Ralph Nader ran on the Green Party ticket in the election of 2000. This was a very close election for the major party candidates George W. Bush and Al Gore. Gore supporters credit the Nader candidacy for its loss of Florida and the 2000 election. The Tea Party has become a major force as part of the Republican Party. The Tea Party platform provides a more conservative agenda than mainline Republicans; however, it remains to be seen if a Tea Party candidate could have a significant-enough coalition to be elected president.

9 CONGRESS

The United States of America essentially grew out of Congress. The original thirteen colonies banded together in what was known as the First Continental Congress. The purpose of the First Continental Congress was simply to approach the king of England for a redress of grievances. The colonists saw themselves as subjects of the king and simply wanted their concerns to be addressed. However, the mood quickly changed when the king rejected the demands of the colonists. The unrest in the colonies was met with force on the part of the king. Based on the British response, the colonists established the Second Continental Congress. What emerged from the Second Continental Congress was the Declaration of Independence. After the Revolutionary War, the new nation was established under the Articles of Confederation, which proclaimed a United States in Congress assembled. In replacing the Articles of Confederation, the new Constitution gave evidence that Congress was to be the central force in the new nation. More attention to detail was given to Congress in Article I of the Constitution than was given to any other branch or aspect of government. This has led some to refer to Congress as the first branch of government.

As discussed in Chapter Two, the bicameral structure of Congress was reached by the Connecticut Compromise between the Virginia Plan and the New Jersey Plan. The House of Representatives is based on the Virginia Plan. The Senate's emphasis on equal representation is based on the New Jersey Plan, while emphasis on representation based on population is based on the Virginia Plan. A decennial census was established for reapportionment purposes in the House of Representatives.

Article I, Section 1 of the Constitution states, "All legislative Powers herein granted shall be vested in a Congress of the United States, which shall consist of a Senate and a House of Representatives." The minimum age to be a member of the House of Representatives is twenty-five, while the minimum age to be a senator is thirty. Each house of Congress has a very distinct structure and area of responsibility. The House of Representatives has the power to bring impeachments. The Senate has the power to try impeachments. The Chief Justice of the Supreme Court presides over impeachments. According to Article I, "all bills raising revenue" must originate in the House of Representatives. The colonists rebelled against the Crown, in part, on the basis of "taxation without representation." Consequently, it was logical that the issue of taxation would be placed closest to the people.

The Senate was designated as the upper chamber by the writers of the Constitution. The structure of the Senate gives evidence that senators were intended to be somewhat removed from day to day politics. Each senator is to serve a six-year term as opposed to a two-year term for House members. Senators were initially elected by state legislators instead of a popular vote. This arrangement mimicked the Electoral College process for electing a president. Under the Articles of Confederation, the president was elected by Congress. Clearly, the writers of the Constitution believed that Senators were to be of a higher calling and, therefore, selected more carefully. It was not until 1913 that the Seventeenth Amendment was ratified, calling for the popular election of senators. The Senate is also given the power of "advice and consent" to the president. This practice is used in the confirmation of executive nominations and the ratification of treaties. Most executive nominations to the federal bureaucracy and federal judiciary must be confirmed by the Senate. Treaties entered into by the president must also be ratified by the Senate to become the law of the land. One of the more famous treaties signed by a president but not ratified by the Senate was the Treaty of Versailles at the end of World War I. The main purpose of this treaty was the creation of the

League of Nations. President Woodrow Wilson signed this treaty, but it was rejected by the U.S. Senate.

There are two major concepts used for analyzing both members of Congress and the Constitutional structure of Congress. These two concepts are ***trustee*** and ***delegate***. This useful distinction can be traced to Burke's Dilemma posited by Edmund Burke. Trustee theory is the idea that a member of Congress will exercise his or her own best judgment regarding legislation in order to promote that which is best for the country as a whole. Often this will put the senator or representative at odds with his or her immediate constituency within the home state or district. Delegate theory is the idea that a member of Congress will vote and sponsor legislation in line with what his or her constituents would like to see happen. The member of Congress who acts as a delegate sees himself or herself as an ambassador for their particular constituency. Delegate theory representation makes it more difficult to achieve compromise or bipartisan outcomes on major pieces of legislation.

The bicameral structure of Congress also has an inherent trustee/delegate theme. The House of Representatives is structured on the delegate model. Representatives only have two-year terms. Brief two year term require that the representative to keep close tabs on his or her constituency. Representatives were not meant to be above the day to day political fray. Moreover, members of the House represent districts not states. There is a smaller geographical area for which a member of the House is responsible. Once again, the design trends more toward a delegate model than a trustee model. Members of the Senate experience the trustee model. Senators are given six-year terms. This is closer to a decade to serve. Clearly, the six-year term was meant to insulate Senators from the day to day political fray. Senators also have the "Advice and Consent" function to the executive as stated in the Constitution. This is carried out in terms of confirmation of presidential nominations to executive positions or to the federal bench. "Advice and Consent" is also carried out in terms of ratification of treaties. A president may negotiate and sign a treaty with another country or countries, but the respective treaty does not become the law of the land or become binding on the United States until it is ratified by the Senate.

LEGISLATIVE SYMMETRY: HOW AN IDEA BECOMES LAW

Article I, Section 7 sets the process by which a bill becomes law:

> *All Bills for raising Revenue shall originate in the House of Representatives; but the Senate may propose or concur with Amendments as on other Bills.*
>
> *Every Bill which shall have passed the House of Representatives and the Senate, shall, before it become a Law, be presented to the President of the United States: If he approve he shall sign it, but if not he shall return it, with his Objections to that House in which it shall have originated, who shall enter the Objections at large on their Journal, and proceed to reconsider it. If after such Reconsideration two thirds of that House shall agree to pass the Bill, it shall be sent, together with the Objections, to the other House, by which it shall likewise be reconsidered, and if approved by two thirds of that House, it shall become a Law. But in all such Cases the Votes of both Houses shall be determined by yeas and Nays, and the Names of the Persons voting for and against the Bill shall be entered on the Journal of each House respectively. If any Bill shall not be returned by the President within ten Days (Sundays excepted) after it shall have been presented to him, the Same shall be a Law, in like Manner as if he had signed it, unless the Congress by their Adjournment prevent its Return, in which Case it shall not be a Law.*
>
> *Every Order, Resolution, or Vote to which the Concurrence of the Senate and House of Representatives may be necessary (except on a question of Adjournment) shall be presented to the President of the United States; and before the Same shall take Effect, shall be approved by him, or being disapproved by him, shall be repassed by two thirds of the Senate and House*

of Representatives, according to the Rules and Limitations prescribed in the Case of a Bill.[1]

Table 9.1

House of Representatives	Senate
Standing Committee	Standing Committee
Subcommittee	Subcommittee
Standing Committee	Standing Committee
Rules Committee	
Floor: Debate, Amendments, Vote	Floor: Debate, Amendments, Vote
Conference Committee	
Floor: Final Vote	Floor: Final Vote
PRESIDENT	

Table 9.1 represents the basic structure of how a bill or an idea becomes law. First, the measure is introduced into Congress through a standing committee. All bills, except tax revenue bills, can begin in either the House or the Senate. A bill may be introduced in the Senate and then sent to the House, or it can be introduced in the House and then sent to the Senate. A bill can be introduced simultaneously in both Houses. Once the bill clears the standing committee, it is then sent to a subcommittee. In the subcommittee additional hearings are held on the legislation as well as mark-ups. Mark-ups are essentially rewrites of the legislation. This is one of the major areas where interested parties attempt to have their interests written into the legislation under consideration. Once a bill clears the subcommittee, it is returned to the full standing committee for additional hearings. In the House of Representatives, the next step is for the measure to be sent to the Rules Committee. The Rules Committee is a permanent standing committee in the House responsible for attaching rules of debate to the measure at hand. The rule determines the length of time the bill will be considered. The rule will also determine how much time each House member will be given to debate the measure on the House floor. In addition, the rule will determine if amendments will be considered and what types

1 Copyright in the Public Domain.

of amendments will be considered. There are basically two types of amendments: ***germane*** and ***non-germane***. Germane amendments are amendments that are added in order to address similar concerns in similar subject matters. Non-germane amendments may address any area other than the piece of legislation under consideration.

Beyond legislation, Congress also passes resolutions. There are joint resolutions and concurrent resolutions. Joint resolutions have the force of law and require either the president's signature or veto. One of the more famous resolutions in the American political narrative is The Tonkin Gulf Resolution. The Tonkin Gulf Resolution of 1964 was nearly passed unanimously. It was the legal authority that paved the way for President Johnson to lead the United States deeper into the Vietnam War.

CONGRESSIONAL COMMITTEES

Congressional committees form the backbone of Congress. Generally, most of the work of Congress takes place in committees. As stated earlier, mark-ups take place within committees. Hearings also take place within committees. Moreover, committees also play an indispensable role in the legislative process. The following are the major types of committees in Congress: standing committees, subcommittees, joint committees, and conference committees. The Rules Committee exists only in the House of Representatives.

Standing committees are the major committees in Congress. There are twenty-five standing committees in the House of Representatives and sixteen in the Senate. Standing committees are permanent committees that exist from Congress to Congress.

House Standing Committees

- Agriculture
- Appropriations

- Armed Services
- Budget
- Education and the Workforce
- Energy and Commerce
- Ethics
- Financial Services
- Foreign Affairs
- Homeland Security
- House Administration
- Judiciary
- Natural Resources
- Oversight and Government Reform
- Rules
- Science, Space, and Technology
- Small Business
- Transportation and Infrastructure
- Veterans' Affairs
- Ways and Means
- Intelligence
- Joint Economic Committee
- Joint Committee on the Library
- Joint Committee on Printing
- Joint Committee on Taxation[2]

Senate Standing Committees

- Agriculture, Nutrition, and Forestry
- Appropriations
- Armed Services
- Banking, Housing, and Urban Affairs
- Budget
- Commerce, Science, and Transportation
- Energy and Natural Resources

2 Copyright in the Public Domain (http://www.house.gov/).

- Environment and Public Works
- Finance
- Foreign Relations
- Health, Education, Labor, and Pensions
- Homeland Security and Governmental Affairs
- Judiciary
- Rules and Administration
- Small Business and Entrepreneurship
- Veterans' Affairs [3]

Joint committees are composed of both members of the House and Senate. A joint committee reports on investigative issues affecting the federal government and pressing issues for the country. The ***Rules Committee*** is unique to the House of Representatives. Unlike the Senate, debate in the House of Representative is not unlimited. Therefore, the Rules Committee is charged with setting the parameters of debate surrounding legislation. Rules attached by the Rules Committee can facilitate or hinder passage of passage of legislation. Another important committee is the ***Conference Committee***. The Conference Committee is composed of members of both parties from both the House of Representatives and the Senate. Members of Congress who are chosen to serve on the Conference Committee are usually members who worked the most on the bill at hand. The purpose of the Conference Committee is to reconcile the House and Senate versions of the same piece of legislation in order to produce a single bill that will be voted on by the House and Senate.

The standing committees all have special oversight and input into their respective areas of responsibility. Some fill the constitutional function of "advice and consent" as it relates to confirmation and ratification politics. For example, during the Watergate crisis, the ***House Judiciary Committee*** voted to impeach President Nixon. However, it could not be seen as a House vote until the entire House had voted on the issue. President Nixon resigned before the entire House voted, thus becoming the first and only president to resign the office. The ***Senate Judiciary Committee*** was embroiled in a bitter battle to confirm

3 Copyright in the Public Domain (http://www.senate.gov/committees_home.htm).

Clarence Thomas to the Supreme Court. Vice President Joe Biden was in the Senate at the time and chaired the Senate Judiciary Committee. The ***Senate Foreign Relations Committee*** is tasked with confirmation of diplomats, the Secretary of State, and the Secretary of Defense. In addition to this, the Senate has to ratify treaties in order for their provisions to become law in the United States.

CONGRESS BY THE NUMBERS

House: 435, 218, 290
Senate: 100, 51, 67, 60

There are three important numbers to consider when talking about the House of Representatives. First, there are 435 representatives. Each represents one district. Consequently, one can view the United States as 435 districts. As a republic, this view of the United States coincides with James Madison's view of the United States as expressed in Federalist #10. In order to pass legislation in the House, there must be a simple majority of 218 votes. This is based on the vote of a full House of Representatives. The Constitution calls for a two-thirds vote of the House of Representatives in order to propose constitutional amendments or override a presidential veto. A two-thirds vote of the House of Representatives requires 290 votes. The number 290 is not a constitutional number. It is simply based on the number of Representatives currently established in the House. The Constitution did set a formula for the number of Representatives. However, if this formula were followed to the letter, the number of representatives in the House would be unmanageable.

There are four important numbers to consider when talking about the Senate. First, there are 100 Senators. The Constitution provides for two Senators per state. Fifty-one constitutes a simple majority in the Senate. A simple majority is required for passage of most legislation, ratify treaties, or confirm presidential nominees to the federal courts or executive branch positions. The number sixty-seven denotes a constitutional majority in the Senate. This is the number of votes needed to propose constitutional amendments, override presidential vetoes, or convict a president after impeachment. Sixty represents what is called a super majority. Sixty votes ensure what is called a filibuster proof majority given the fact that sixty votes are needed to end a filibuster.

10 THE PRESIDENT

Article II of the U.S. Constitution states "[the] Executive power shall be vested in a President of the United States of America." Article II also states that this individual "... take care that the Laws be faithfully executed ..." From a reading of Article II of the Constitution, it is possible to extract a portrait of the powers and responsibility of the president. First, it is understood that the President serves as the ***chief administrator***. The writers of the Constitution took care to make sure that another king was not being created; however, it is understood that there is a single executive. The president is also the ***commander in chief*** of America's armed forces. This includes a wide range of military options such as the Navy, Marines, Army, and Air Force. The Air Force is subject to presidential authority by definition given the fact that there was no Air Force at the time the Constitution was written. On the other hand, one must remain mindful that only Congress can declare war. The president also serves as the ***chief domestic policy leader***. The Constitution states that from time to time the president must "give to the Congress Information of the State of the Union, and recommend to their Consideration such Measures [as shall be judged] necessary and expedient." The president is also the ***chief foreign policy actor***. As a consequence of this position as chief foreign policy actor, the president formulates America's foreign policy. The writers of the Constitution made this clear by granting the president the authority to make treaties with the "advice and consent" of Congress. Other responsibilities of the president have been added through custom and practice. The president serves as the ***chief symbol of the nation***. In this capacity, the president leads the nation in mourning after tragic loss of life that affects the nation. The president also represents the nation abroad in state funerals honoring deceased heads of state from other countries. Although political parties were not clearly formed when George Washington was president, the U.S. President has emerged as the ***leader of the president's party***. As the leader of the party, the president is sometimes seen as the campaigner and fund raiser in chief. Many times, this expectation follows the president long after the person leaves office.

In order to gain a full view of the American presidency, it is necessary to study the office by cross referencing the president's roles and power with the practice of individuals who have held the office. For example George Washington, who served as the nation's first president under the current Constitution, had a blank slate upon which to operate. Washington is credited with establishing precedence or a blueprint for subsequent holders of the office. One of lasting legacies of Washington was the two-term presidency. The Constitution stated that the president's term of office would be four years, but placed on limitations on how many terms a president could serve. George Washington served two terms and retired from office. This pattern was closely followed by subsequent presidents until Franklin Roosevelt. President Roosevelt was elected to the office of President four times. This prompted the ratification of the Twenty-second Amendment to the Constitution in 1951, which states, "No person shall be elected to the office of President more than twice, and no person who has held the office of President for more than two years of a term to which some other person was elected President shall be elected to the office more than once."

Franklin Roosevelt was elected to the office of president during the Great Depression. He defeated Herbert Hoover in the election of 1932. Franklin Roosevelt was elected in November of 1932 but was not sworn in to office, as directed by the Constitution, until March 4, 1933. This prompted the ratification of the ratification of the Twentieth Amendment to the Constitution in 1933. The Twentieth Amendment, also known as the "Lame Duck" Amendment, moved the presidential inaugural date from March 4 to January 20. This was to ensure a more rapid change in administrations from the outgoing to the incoming president.

President Roosevelt is credited with saving the United States from economic collapse. President Lincoln is credited with saving the United States from utter destruction. By the time Abraham Lincoln was sworn in as president on March 4, 1861, many of the southern states had seceded from the union known as the United States of America. The tumultuous Civil War ensued. A central issue of the Civil War was the enslavement people of African descent. Closely associated with the enslavement issue was the argument surrounding states' rights. Lincoln's actions during this particular period were focused on saving the Union. Although he was intent on saving the Union, one can argue that several of his actions were unconstitutional. For example, the vaulted Emancipation Proclamation was unconstitutional in that it sought to liberate the southern planters' property without due process of law as contained in the Fifth Amendment. The property in question consisted of the Africans who were enslaved.

Lincoln's actions have been characterized as presidential prerogative. John Locke expounded on the theory of presidential prerogative in his ***Two Treatises of Government.*** According to Locke's theory, the president has the power to act for the good of the country in the absence of Congress or at times against the prescriptions of Congress. Other theories of the presidency include stewardship theory and constitutional theory. Theodore Roosevelt advocated stewardship theory in the *Autobiography of Theodore Roosevelt* published in 1913. Stewardship theory proposes that the president is permitted to act as long as the actions are not prohibited by the Constitution. Constitutional theory, as advocated by William Howard Taft in *Our Chief Magistrate and His Powers*, takes a more conservative position on power. Taft argued that the president can only act where such actions are granted by the Constitution. Consequently, constitutional theory places a great deal of emphasis on enumerated powers. Enumerated powers are simply those that are listed in the Constitution.

THE ELECTORAL COLLEGE

Every four years America engages in a significant debate concerning the Electoral College. On one side of the spectrum there are those who advocate for a popular vote that would be more democratic. Those who argue for the status quo believe that a popular vote would spawn too many minor parties that are not serious contenders for the office of president. The Electoral College was designed to ensure that the correct person would secure the presidency. It is one of those less than democratic aspects of the Constitution that was incorporated to place a check on the people. As designed by the writers of the Constitution, electors elect the president and not the people. The Electoral College is composed of the size of a state's congressional delegation plus three electors assigned to Washington, D.C. This makes a total of 538 electors in the Electoral College. It is possible for a presidential candidate to have a majority of the popular vote yet lose the presidential election. In the election of 1876, Samuel Tilden had a majority of the popular vote but lost the presidency to Rutherford B. Hayes in the Electoral College. This was also the case in the election of 2000. In one of the more contentious elections in the American political narrative, Al Gore, President Clinton's vice president, won the popular vote, but George W. Bush won the presidency in the Electoral College.

DOMESTIC POLICY

As stated earlier, the Constitution requires the president to inform Congress concerning the State of the Union and to make recommendations to Congress related to policy. One of the primary ways in which the president advises Congress is through the submission of the budget. The budget is a very political document. The president submits the budget to Congress summarizing the President's priorities for the upcoming fiscal year. Congress, in turn, goes through the budget in order to determine areas of agreement and areas of needed compromise. Congress's concern also centers on spending for senators' and representatives' states and districts. Consequently, there are times when Congress wants to spend more than the president, and there are times when the president wants to spend less than Congress. President Nixon used impoundment in order to curtail spending. Impoundment is the process of ordering agencies and offices not to spend money that that been authorized by Congress to spend. As a reaction to the impoundment policies of Richard Nixon, Congress passed the Congressional Budget and Impoundment Control Act of 1974. The act required the president to inform Congress of which funds were to be impounded. Congress would decide if it could agree with impoundment or not. President Nixon vetoed the legislation but Congress overrode the President's veto.

Different aspects of the budget have come to the forefront during different administrations. By the time Ronald Reagan became president, deficit reduction was the central focus of Congress and the president. Deficit reduction translated into a reduction in the size of government. Shrinking the size of government was President Reagan's way of "getting government off the backs of the people." A plan was developed to bring the deficit down to zero in six years. The legislation that embodied this plan was known as the Balanced Budget and Emergency Deficit Control Act of 1985. A central component of this legislation was Congress's power of sequestration. Simply stated, if the president's budget did not meet deficit reduction targets, Congress could order that funds should not be spent. This law was declared unconstitutional in Bowser v. Synar in 1986 based on the legislative veto contained within the legislation. According to the Supreme Court, the law violated the constitutional process of presentment, which provides the executive an opportunity to sign or reject legislative actions. Irrespective of the attempts to reduce the deficit, it grew at a very rapid pace for the next few years.

The president and Congress have been presented with an "invitation to struggle" over both domestic and foreign policy. The Balanced Budget and Emergency Deficit Control Act was but one attempt of many to give either the president or Congress additional authority over the budget. Another such attempt was the attempt to grant the president the line item veto similar to that used by various governors across the country. The line item veto had been a favorite topic of discussion on the part the Republican Party during the Clinton administration. The law was passed in Clinton's first term but could not go into effect until after the upcoming election. Given the fact that Clinton defeated Bob Dole to secure a second term, he was the first to use the line item veto. His use of the veto to deny funds to New York City was the basis for a lawsuit filed on behalf of the City of New York. The Supreme Court eventually ruled the president's use of the line item veto unconstitutional. In this case, Clinton v. City of New York, the Supreme Court ruled that the line item veto was not in harmony with the Constitution due to the constitutional requirement that the president sign or veto an entire bill and not just part of a bill.

FOREIGN POLICY

Many of the largest battles over policy occur between the president and Congress regarding foreign policy. The Constitution essentially guarantees this perpetual struggle between Congress and the president. Article I of the Constitution states that only Congress has the power to declare war. On the other hand, Article II of the Constitution states that the president is the commander-in-chief of the nation's armed forces. The Vietnam War posed particular problems for Congress and the president in regard to war powers. In 1964 Congress passed the ***Tonkin Gulf Resolution*** authorizing President Johnson to take whatever measures necessary to conduct military operations in Southeast Asia. The troop levels quickly increased to close to 500,000 on the ground in Vietnam. Notwithstanding America's military commitment, the South Vietnamese government soon fell to North Vietnam. Prior to the end of the war Congress passed the ***War Powers Resolution*** over President Nixon's veto in 1973. Although it was a de jure attempt on the part of the Congress to rein in the president's war making propensities, the law, in fact, gave the president a sixty-day window in which to introduce American forces into areas of hostility.

Subsequent to the War Powers Resolution, the president and Congress have attempted to reach a compromise on the use of the military. The nature of compromise is the president will come to Congress and make a strong case as to why the U.S. military would need to be used. If Congress is persuaded by the president's argument, Congress will vote in order to authorize the use of military force (AUMF). This process has been used on three occasions. The first was AUMF 1991, which gave President George H. W. Bush the authority to fight against Saddam Hussein who had invaded Kuwait. The second use was AUMF 2001, which was an authorization for George W. Bush to use military force against terror. The war in Afghanistan began under this authorization. The third and most controversial AUMF was granted in 2002. This was the authorization to use military force against Iraq. Shortly after the authorization was given, the war in Iraq began in March 2003. Although President Obama has been heavily engaged in Syria, there has not been a clear vote for AUMF in Syria. The reason for this is that the objective continues to change. Late in 2013, the debate centered around AUMF against the Assad regime due to the use of chemical weapons. Late in 2014, the debate centered around AUMF against the Islamic State in Iraq and Syria (ISIS).

THE U.S. PRESIDENT ENGAGES THE WORLD

Not only is the American president seen as the leader of the United States, the president is also seen as a world leader. In this capacity four U.S. presidents have received the Nobel Peace Prize. The four presidential recipients are: Theodore Roosevelt, Woodrow Wilson, Jimmy Carter, and Barack Obama.

> ***Theodore Roosevelt:*** *1906 for Russo-Japanese War mediation.*
>
> ***Woodrow Wilson:*** *1919 for helping to establish the League of Nations.*
>
> ***Jimmy Carter:*** *2002 for global advancement of human rights.*
>
> ***Barack Obama:*** *2009 for emphasis on international diplomacy.*

The irony of these American presidents winning the Nobel Peace Prize is that they tended to receive more praise from the world community than from their own constituents. Woodrow Wilson basically died a broken individual after the U.S. Senate failed to ratify the Treaty of Versailles, which would have resulted in the United States joining the League of Nations. Jimmy Carter was a one-term president. He was humiliated by the hostage crisis that resulted from the 1979 Iranian Revolution. When Carter was defeated by Reagan, he was seen as weak and ineffective. When Barack Obama won the prize in 2009, many Americans began to question the validity of the Nobel Prize Committee. Lowering the prospect of war temperature on an international scale was not seen as an achievement.

All U.S. presidents have had to find the right balance between domestic and foreign policy. At times foreign policy considerations have derailed what a president wanted to accomplish domestically. One of more noted cases of this issue has to do with Lyndon Johnson's Great Society/War on Poverty being derailed by the war in Vietnam. Jimmy Carter's energy concerns essentially tied domestic and foreign policy into a seamless concern. The turbulence of civil rights and the Soviet Union kept John F. Kennedy walking a fine balance between peaceful resolve and catastrophe. Ronald Reagan lost focus on the economy due to the Iran-Contra scandal. Richard Nixon will be less remembered for his overtures to China than for Watergate. Harry Truman dropped the atomic bomb on Hiroshima and Nagasaki, but he also integrated the U.S. military. Franklin Roosevelt struck the right balance between the Great Depression and World War II. He redefined the presidency in many ways. Barack Obama has become a natural presidential heir to Franklin Roosevelt in attempting to strike the proper balance between monumental foreign policy issues and extremely poignant domestic policy concerns.

11 THE BUREAUCRACY

Hurricane Katrina battered the Gulf Shore states of America in 2005, leaving a trail of destruction from the pan handle of Florida to Louisiana. The most devastating story from Hurricane Katrina, however, relates to the events that happened in New Orleans. The city was flooded and many thousands of people were displaced. Shocking images captured the desperation of people who were stranded at the New Orleans Superdome without food or water. The government agency that was to deal with such disasters became part of the news story itself. The Federal Emergency Management Agency (FEMA) was seen as ineffective and essentially as contributing to the disaster rather than bringing assistance to those who were most affected by the storm.

This is not the first time that FEMA has made the news for something other than offering assistance in the wake of a natural or manmade disaster. During the Congressional hearings on the Iran-Contra Affair, the question of FEMA's efficacy was raised during the testimony of Lieutenant Colonel Oliver North. Senator Tom Harkin asked North if there were plans to suspend the Constitution under FEMA. Harkin was immediately admonished by the committee chair, Senator Inouye, not to discuss this topic in open session.

The supreme irony concerning FEMA's response to Katrina is that the agency was a part of the massive government reorganization that occurred in 2002 as a part of the Homeland Security Act of 2002. The law was passed in response to the 2001 attacks on the United

States. The new law was the most massive reorganization of government since the National Security Act of 1947.

Article II, Section 1, Paragraph 8 of the Constitution contains the presidential oath of office. In the oath, the president pledges to "faithfully execute the Office of President." Article II, Section 3, Paragraph 1 of the Constitution charges the president to "take care that the laws be faithfully executed." It is through the bureaucracy that the president executes the laws. At the pinnacle of the bureaucracy is the President's Cabinet, which consists of fifteen Departments. Table 11.1 lists the fifteen departments along with each department's date of creation and the president under whom the department was created.

Table 11.1

CABINET LEVEL DEPARTMENT	DATE CREATED	PRESIDENT WHEN CREATED
Department of State	July 27, 1789	George Washington
Department of Treasury	September 2, 1789	George Washington
Department of Justice	September 24, 1789	George Washington
Department of War	August 1789	George Washington
Interior	March 3, 1849	Zachary Taylor
Agriculture	May 15, 1862	Grover Cleveland
Department of Commerce & Labor	1903	Theodore Roosevelt
Department of Commerce	March 4, 1913	Woodrow Wilson
Department of Labor	March 4, 1913	Woodrow Wilson
Department of Defense	August 10, 1949	Harry Truman
Department of Health, Education & Welfare	April 11, 1953	Dwight Eisenhower
Department of Housing & Urban Development (HUD)	September 9, 1965	Lyndon Johnson
Department of Transportation	October 16, 1966	Lyndon Johnson
Department of Energy	August 4, 1977	Jimmy Carter
Department of Health & Human Services	September 27, 1979	Jimmy Carter
Department of Education	September 27, 1979	Jimmy Carter
Department of Veteran Affairs	October 25, 1988	Ronald Reagan
Department of Homeland Security	November 25, 2002	George W. Bush

A careful look at the President's Cabinet provides a political narrative that addresses some of the country's highest priorities over time. The original Cabinet consisted of four departments. The Departments of State and Treasury were headed by Thomas Jefferson and Alexander Hamilton, respectively. It was from these two departments that the country's two-party system emerged. Jefferson was more interested in an active foreign policy while Washington wanted to foster neutrality. Hamilton promoted the idea of a national bank that eventually evolved into our current Federal Reserve System. Today, the Department of War is known as the Department of Defense. Issues surrounding the Department of War led to the first impeachment of a president.

Although America has only a single executive, the president is not alone in carrying out the law. Consequently, there is a bureaucracy in place that facilitates the carrying out of the law. At the core of the bureaucracy is the President's Cabinet. The Cabinet currently consists of fifteen department-level organizations. The fifteen departments are: the Departments of State, Treasury, Justice, Defense, Agriculture, Labor, Transportation, Housing and Urban Development, Health and Human Services, Education, Energy, Veteran Affairs, and Homeland Security. The departments came into existence at different points in time and were created in order to address major issues as well as to service a particular constituency. The first two departments were the Department of State and the Department of Treasury. The most recent department to be created is the Department of Homeland Security.

The Department of Homeland Security was created after the terrorist attack of September 11, 2001. It served as the largest reorganization of government since the creation of the Defense Department in 1947 with the National Security Act of 1947. The Defense Department was once known as the Department of War. The National Security Act of 1947 also created the Central Intelligence Agency (CIA). In addition, the National Security Act also created the National Security Council, which advises the president closely on foreign policy issues. Just as the Homeland Security Act has been designed to prepare and protect the nation regarding terrorism, the National Security Act was designed to engage the Soviet Union during the Cold War.

The 1973 oil embargo on the part of OPEC (Organization of Petroleum Exporting Countries) sent the United States into an energy crisis. One of the earliest responses of the American government was the 1974 Emergency Highway Energy Conservation Act. The law, which was administered by the Department of Transportation, provided a maximum national highway speed of 55 m.p.h. Although the law was relaxed in the late 1980s, the 55 m.p.h. speed is still very visible on highways around the country. The crisis extended into the administration of Jimmy Carter. President Carter referred to America's attempt at energy independence as the "moral equivalence of war." Consequently, the Department of Energy was created during the Carter administration in order to spearhead America's efforts at energy conservation. Ironically, Ronald Reagan campaigned on eliminating the Department of Energy. Texas Governor Rick Perry made his famous gaff during the Republican Primary presidential debate when he was unable to remember that the Department of Energy was one the Departments he would eliminate if elected to the office of president.

Agencies, Bureaus, and Commissions

Most Americans relate to the American government through the identification of their representatives in Congress and, from time to time, through identifying with the president. However, it is through the bureaucracy that most Americans interact with the government. This is particularly true of agencies, bureaus, and commissions. Almost every aspect of an American citizen's life is touched through one of these types of government entities. For example, the public regularly encounters the ***Transportation Safety Administration (TSA)***. A brief visit to tsa.gov reveals the essential information concerning the creation of the TSA:

> *The Aviation and Transportation Security Act, passed by the 107th Congress and signed on November 19, 2001, established TSA and required the completion of more than 30 mandates by the end of 2002. In the largest civilian undertaking in the history of the United States, TSA met each one of these initial requirements including:*

Assuming responsibility for all civil aviation security functions from the Federal Aviation Administration.

Hiring, training and deploying security officers for over 400 commercial airports from Guam to Alaska in 12 months.

Providing 100 percent screening of all checked baggage for explosives by December 31,2002. In March 2003, TSA transferred from the Department of Transportation to the Department of Homeland Security which was created on November 25, 2002 by the Homeland Security Act of 2002 unifying the nation's response to threats to the homeland.[1]

The TSA often makes the news based on the latest body search techniques that will be employed at airports. Some are considered more intrusive than others. There is also the privacy issue that is raised concerning full body scanners. Nevertheless, it is a major task to attempt to keep airports and air travel safe. In late 2014 a new threat revealed that there are potential hazards yet to be address. The necessity for screening for the Ebola virus revealed that despite the best security apparatus, unanticipated tragedies can place a heavy burden on the government's ability to respond.

Just as the TSA touches the lives of millions of Americans each day, so do many of the other agencies of the government. The ***Federal Bureau of Investigation (FBI)*** is the government's principal crime unit. The FBI is called upon to investigate all manner of issues once they are raised to a federal level. The ***Secret Service***, as a unit of the Treasury Department, is charged with protecting the president. The ***Internal Revenue Service (IRS)*** is known for collecting taxes. It is a rare individual who does not think about the IRS during April of each year. Anyone who uses any type of phone, a garage door opener, goes online, or watches any type of television encounters the ***Federal Communications Commission (FCC)*** on a minute-by-minute basis. The FCC regulates not only frequencies and bandwidth, but also what we see and hear via various media sources.

1 Copyright in the Public Domain (http://www.tsa.gov/about-tsa/history).

The alphabet soup (FBI, CIA, NSA, ATF, IRS, SEC, FCC, FDA, TSA, NASA, FEC, NTSB, OSHA, EEOC, FDIC, TVA, NSF, NLRB) of the federal bureaucracy is quite extensive. The aforementioned list of agencies and commissions is not meant to be an exhaustive list. However, its limited purpose is to present a small demonstration of the extensive nature of government and how it touches nearly every aspect of life in the United States. Based on this reality, some argue for more government while others argue for less government. There are even those who argue for no government. In many ways the government facilitates our lives. At its worst, government can be intrusive and serve as a hindrance to the achievement of one's goals. All in all it is the American government and it is possible to petition it for a redress of grievances.

PRESIDENTIAL CONTROL OF THE BUREAUCRACY

Article II, Section 2, Paragraph 2 of the Constitution states the following:

> *He shall have Power, by and with the Advice and Consent of the Senate, to make Treaties, provided two thirds of the Senators present concur; and he shall nominate, and by and with the Advice and Consent of the Senate, shall appoint Ambassadors, other public Ministers and Consuls, Judges of the supreme Court, and all other Officers of the United States, whose Appointments are not herein otherwise provided for, and which shall be established by Law: but the Congress may by Law vest the Appointment of such inferior Officers, as they think proper, in the President alone, in the Courts of Law, or in the Heads of Departments.*[2]

2 Copyright in the Public Domain.

The Constitution was clear on the president's appointment power to the bureaucracy; however, debates arose as to the president's removal power. This debate was quite evident in the creation of the first Cabinet under George Washington. Some members of Congress acquiesced in the constitutional assurance of the president's appointment power but wanted to include provisions in the creation of departments that would curtail the president's removal authority. James Madison stated that such authority would be a major encroachment of power on the part of Congress. According to Madison, "... if the Legislature has a power, such as contended for, they may subject and transfer at discretion powers from one department of our government to another; they may, on that principle, exclude the President altogether from exercising any authority in the removal of officers; they may give it to the Senate alone, or the President and Senate combined."[3]

The first impeachment came over a battle between Congress and president regarding removal power. President Lincoln's assassination altered the course of post-African enslavement and the process of Reconstruction. Upon becoming president, Andrew Johnson, Lincoln's vice president, sought to take a more moderate regarding the reintegration of the southern rebellious states into the Union. Understanding President Andrew Johnson's position, Congress sought a method to prevent Johnson from unraveling the government's attention to Reconstruction. As a consequence, Congress passed the Tenure of Office Act of 1867. The law sought to prevent President Johnson from derailing Reconstruction efforts by preventing him from removing key members of the executive branch. When Andrew Johnson sought to removed Secretary of War Edward Stanton from office, Congress impeached Andrew Johnson. He was acquitted in the Senate trial. The act was eventually found to be unconstitutional.

George W. Bush pushed what has been called the "unitary executive." ***Unitary executive theory*** is the belief that the president is the head of the executive branch and therefore should control every aspect of the executive branch with little interference from Congress. The scope of the president's authority reaches all agencies, commissions,

---

3 Michael Nelson, ed. *The Evolving Presidency: Landmark Documents, 1787–2010.* Washington, D.C.: CQ Press, p.47.

and bureaus. Although not limited to the idea of unitary executive, issuance of ***executive orders*** constitutes a major way in which the president seeks to control the bureaucracy. An executive order is simply a directive from the office of the president pertaining to presidential initiatives. Executive orders do not require the approval of Congress.[4] Examples of executive orders include:

> *Harry Truman: E.O. 9981 integrated U.S. Military*
>
> *John F. Kennedy: E.O. 10925 urged "affirmative action" among government contractors*
>
> *Barack Obama: E.O. 13493 initiated review of Detention Policies at Guantanamo Bay*

President Truman's executive order brought about racial integration of the military. Many wanted President Obama to open the military to homosexuals through Executive Order. However, President Obama chose to bring change through legislation. President Kennedy's executive order was one of the earliest expressions of "affirmative action." President Obama sought to close the Guantanamo Bay Detention Facility through executive order, but the facility has remained open throughout his administration.

George W. Bush and Barack Obama: Keeping the Faith

The Cabinet-level departments tend to reflect major policy initiatives that the country has undertaken. Elevating concerns to Cabinet-level status indicates the seriousness with which issues are taken. For example, the issue concerning how veterans are treated led to the creation of the Department of Veteran Affairs. The attacks against America on September 11, 2001 led to the creation of the Department of Homeland

4 Joseph A. Pika & John Anthony Maltese, *The Politics of the Presidency*, Rev.Ed., Washington, D.C.: CQ Press, 2014, p. 17.

Security. Such creations of departments reflect concerns at the macro level of government. Entities created through executive order often reflect the micro concerns of individual presidents. The creation of The White House Office of Faith-based and Community Initiatives and The White House Office of Faith-based and Neighborhood Partnerships were created by respective executive orders on the part of President George W. Bush and President Barack Obama. Each demonstrated a commitment to their shared belief in a higher power. Although both entities were faith based, each reflects a slightly different interpretation of the role of faith in a government setting.

President Bush was the first to set forth such an office. It was controversial from the beginning given the First Amendment's separation of church and state. George W. Bush, who also believed in smaller government, believed that churches and community organizations were better suited to deal with social issues than the larger federal government. Consequently, it would be permissible to extend federal funds to such organizations as long as they did not attempt to proselytize when administering assistance to various constituents. The more cynical argued that this was just a political attempt to secure the evangelical base for the Republican Party. Barack Obama's interpretation of faith-based initiatives stemmed from his time as a community organizer. The idea of a partnership was meant to downplay the government side of this endeavor and place more emphasis on the community. Ironically, both expressions have withstood constitutional scrutiny to date. Whether or not future presidents continue to offer support remains to be seen.

12 DOMESTIC AND ECONOMIC POLICY

Domestic and economic policy in the United States encompass a wide range of topics and concerns. This area of policy can also be the most contentious area due to the fact that, unlike foreign policy, Congress and the president often have a shared stake in the outcome. Domestic policy also reveals the differing values of the nation. Nowhere is this reflected more than in the formulation of the budget. The budgetary process is an essential part of governing. Both congressional and presidential roles in the process are clearly defined. Congress has the power of the purse. The president sets the parameters of debate in the State of the Union Address and the subsequently submitted budget.

Economic policy is a major component of domestic policy. The creation of a nationwide economic policy is known as macroeconomic policy. There are two aspects to macroeconomic policy: fiscal policy and monetary policy. Fiscal policy is within the purview of the president and Congress. It pertains to taxation and spending. Monetary policy is the purview of the Federal Reserve System. The central concern is with the money supply and interest rates.

Fiscal policy refers to taxation and spending. This is the prevue of Congress and the executive. In assessing fiscal policy it is necessary to look at the major domestic policy actors in the executive and in Congress. The president serves as the main domestic and economic policy actor. The president submits a budget to Congress. Congress reacts to the president's budget. These procedures were established by the Budget and Accounting Act of 1921. The Bureau of the Budget was also established in order to advise the president on budgetary formation. The Bureau of the Budget was later changed to the Office of Management and Budget (OMB), which is a part of what is known as the Executive Office of the President (EOP). The Executive Office of the President (EOP) was created by the Reorganization Act of 1939. The EOP was established in order to advise the president on the day to day issues related to governing. Another component of EOP is the Council of Economic Advisors (CEA). The CEA advises the president concerning economic trends and forecasts. Committees address the congressional side of fiscal policy. The first committee to consider is the House Ways and Means Committee. The Ways and Means Committee carries out an important constitutional function of Congress. According to the Constitution, "All bills raising revenue shall originate in the House of Representatives ...." The issue of taxation was a major cause of the American Revolution. Therefore, placing the issue of taxation in the House that is closest to the people was a safeguard against "taxation without representation." The Senate Finance Committee mirrors the functions of the House Ways and Means Committee. Other essential Committees include the House and Senate Budget Committees. Another aspect of congressional fiscal policy is the Congressional Budget Office (CBO). The CBO was established by the Congressional Budget and Impoundment Control Act 1974. The CBO was established in order to counter the expertise of the Office of Management, which advises the President.

The Federal Reserve System functions outside fiscal policy. The Federal Reserve System, or The Fed, is concerned with control of the money supply or interest rates. The Fed is necessarily concerned with the politics of the economy. Nevertheless, Fed policy will, at times, attempt to coordinate monetary policy with fiscal policy in order to ward off inflation or recession. A good example of this has been Fed policy during the recession that began to affect the United States during the latter months of 2008. Although the Federal Reserve System was created with the Federal Reserve Act of 1913, the issue of a national bank for the United States began with the creation of the nation. Alexander Hamilton first raised the issue during the administration of

George Washington. The existence the first national bank led to the case McColloch v. Maryland 1819. The state of Maryland attempted to tax the bank. The Supreme Court ruled that the power to tax is the power to destroy. Consequently, no state entity is superior to the federal government.

The Fed controls the money supply through three principal methods. First, there is the prime rate. This is the rate that banks charge one another for loans. An increase in the rate decreases the money supply by causing the price of money to increase. A decrease in the prime rate encourages more lending and places more money in circulation. Second, the Federal Open Market Committee (FOMC) can either sell government securities or buy government securities. Through selling government securities, the Fed takes money out of the economy, which reduces the money supply. By buying securities, money is placed back into the economy. Third, the Fed can increase the Federal Reserve requirement, which is the amount of funds that banks are required to have on reserve relative to a bank's assets. An increase in the reserve requirement takes money out of the economy while relaxing the requirement increases the money supply.

Domestic policy addresses economic and financial concerns directly. Such concerns include unemployment, the safety net, inflation, poverty, wealth creation, and issues concerning economic equality. Nowhere is the issue of inequality placed on a more public display than in our public school systems. All one needs to do is take a look at Detroit public schools where many locations have closed. Those that remain open face financial problems that contribute to a subpar education for the youth of Detroit. This inequality affects many urban and rural school districts across the United States. This is no less true in Buffalo, New York, than it is in Chicago, Illinois.

High dropout rates, high absenteeism, and crime have become common place almost to the point of being accepted as the normal course of education. Ideological battles between conservatives and liberals find expression in public schools. Conservatives propose solutions such as school vouchers for parents in order for them to send their kids to private schools. Many see this as a simple attack on public schools by taking public money away from public schools and channeling it into private schools. The opposition to public schools falls right in line with a general opposition to government or the public sector. At times this opposition also has racial overtones alluding to white suburban tax payers footing the bill for a black urban underclass.

The public versus private battle was on full display during the 2012 election. Republican candidate Mitt Romney's 47 percent comments at a fundraiser gave evidence that the ideological opposition to the government stems more from opposition to a sector of the government that is perceived to aid or assist people of color. The fact that a majority of those who depend on the government are white leads commentators to wonder why working class whites tend to support Republicans in a blatant example of voting against their own interest. African Americans may find themselves disproportionately represented in their positive relationship with the government, but whites are more widely served and dependent on the government. Nevertheless, whites tend to see their interests as different from those of African Americans. Consequently, the public versus private debate also surfaces within the familiar phrases such as "urban versus suburban," "tax payers' dollars," and "the deserving poor versus takers."

America has a capitalist economy. Therefore, a great deal of emphasis is placed on the workings of the free market. Capitalism cannot survive in an absolute free market system. Capitalists also defend government. Government has to create a stable environment that is conducive to growth and new markets. It was government that bailed out the capitalists during the economic collapse of 2008 to the tune of $708 billion. The Bush tax cuts, along with cuts to the social safety net, is an example of government redistributing wealth upwards. Often, this can explain a robust economic recovery while wages are stagnant. Another way in which this dichotomy emerges into popular understanding is the demand for cities to cut funding to school districts and reduce state funding for their institutions of higher learning. Once a state reduces its funding to state colleges, increased costs are passed on to students in the form of higher tuition and fees. This is what happened when college students' grants for education were replaced with more student loans offered by private lenders. A major outcome of this reality has been increased debt for many who seek a higher education.

Private markets must keep expanding and developing new areas for investment. One major place where a great deal of money exists is in

Social Security. George W. Bush campaigned on the need to reform Social Security by allowing individuals to opt out and place their money in the stock market. He claimed that workers could make better decisions with their money than the government. The argument was aimed principally at young professionals who are more likely to favor investing more than older workers already vested in Social Security. Imagine what life would be like now for many Americans if their life savings had been placed in the market during the 2008 collapse of the financial markets in the absence of Social Security.

The public sphere and the private sphere must work in harmony or at least attempt to complement one another. Private enterprise has known many failures. Mitt Romney essentially stated that he wanted to be the Chief Executive Officer (CEO) of the United States. One basic problem with this metaphor is that the United States is not a corporation. America is a country based on the will of the people reified in a government. Destroy the government and you destroy the people.

Many different ideals and ideas compete for primacy in the political realm of the United States. Liberty, equality, and democracy are three of these ideals that garner a great deal of attention. Many argue that our great nation was founded upon these principles. In reality, however, ideals often conflict and, if carried to their logical conclusions, could cancel one another out. Too much liberty cancels out equality. Too much equality cancels out liberty. Moreover, the framers of the Constitution were leery of democracy. Consequently, within the American political sphere, there is a constant balancing act between ideals and a government designed to regulate these ideals. Many times the struggle between these ideals goes undetected. Nevertheless, catch phrases give superficial evidence of deep seated conflicting claims on America. Such phrases include "equal opportunity," "equal pay for equal work," and "government is part of the problem, not the solution."

Recently, attention has been given to the growing income inequality in America as well as the massive gap in wealth between those who have and those who do not have as much. Some even argue that it goes against the ideals for which America stands. Published reports from an updated study by economists Emmanuel Saez and Thomas Piketty point to a growing inequality. The most glaring report states that 10 percent of earners took home over half of the income in the

United States. Add to this the consistent reports that African American and Latino unemployment rates remain higher than the national rate. Women continue to earn less than men. Workers are losing ground as it pertains to benefits and pensions. These hardening trends have led some to argue that this modern or new inequality is a threat to democracy. Contrary to this opinion, one can conclude that America is working just the way it was originally envisioned and, in some respects, designed to work. One need only look at the particular interests that were written into the Constitution.

Rewind to the summer of 1787 and the writing of the Constitution. What was the status of Blacks during the writing of the Constitution and in the immediate aftermath of its ratification? Even white males without sufficient property were looked down upon. As late as 1848 the Declaration of Sentiments revealed the status of women in American society. It was a document that spoke for a group of people who essentially had no rights. The Thirteenth and Fourteenth Amendments had not altered the original Constitution to make African enslavement unconstitutional and provide for "equal protection" under the law. Even the Thirteenth Amendment came with a major "exception." One can conclude that this major exception did not bring about an actual end to enslavement but simply transformed "slavery" into the criminal justice system. Liberty was the dominate theme at the writing of the Constitution. Equality, at that time, was a belief that the states had equal political power as quasi sovereign entities. When Jefferson declared that "all men are created equal," he also said that they were endowed by their Creator with such "inalienable rights" as "liberty." On whose behalf was Jefferson writing? What group of people did he have in mind? The procurement and protection of property were paramount in the minds of those who drew up the framework for this nation. There is no wonder that the Constitution provided for the return of Africans who had sought to escape enslavement by fleeing northward. Moreover, no one denies that the framers of the Constitution were leery of democracy. Consequently, there was instituted an Electoral College to serve as a firewall between the people and the institution of the presidency. Even U.S. Senators were originally elected by state legislators. James Madison argued in Federalist #10 that "the most common and durable source of factions has been the various and unequal distribution of property." According to Madison, liberty is at the heart of this state of affairs. Yet, instead of addressing the economic inequality, Madison wanted to design a government that could preserve liberty, control the people, and ward off the leveling effects of social and economic equality. Madison argued for the regulation of inequality not for its nullification.

There are times when it is not advisable to argue for the original intent of the framers of the Constitution. The progress that has come in American society has come through the unintended loopholes that were created by the framers own words. For example, the beginning to the Preamble to the Constitution reads, "In order to form a more perfect Union ..." Could "more perfect" have meant a more sufficient system of enslavement? Could it have meant a way to maximize profits at the expense of laborers? Perhaps Martin Luther King, Jr.'s use of the phrase "We hold these truths to be self-evident" had a totally different meaning from Thomas Jefferson's use of the same phrase. Nevertheless, it served as a loophole through which the original intent has been significantly challenged and in some cases defeated. Yet, recent reports paint a gloomy picture regarding income inequality. The many conservatives have adopted a wholesale assault on progress that has come through the loopholes. Conservatives consistently recite the mantra of "original intent." Moreover, they have adopted a mantra of less government. Less government, according to this perspective, means a scrapping of the social safety net.

Metaphorically speaking, the progress that came through the loopholes stretched the United States beyond its original intent. Consequently, it is the nature of that which is elastic, once stretched, to try and regain its original form. This is not to say that the original form was a moral form. This is to say, however, that reports of income inequality should come as no surprise. It is difficult to say that income inequality is a threat to democracy given the fact that is questionable as to whether America is a democracy or a Madisonian Republic. Persistent inequality, on the other hand, is a threat to the very people who find themselves victims of an unfettered liberty. Nevertheless, there are some in this country who forcefully advocate against those who have less. They, in turn, promote the alleviation of any financial constraints or restraints on the interests of the very wealthy defined as being in the interest of liberty.

13 FOREIGN POLICY

President Barack Obama received a personal phone call from Russian President Vladimir Putin in March of 2014. While the world will have to wait for the exact transcript of the conversation, it is known that it was made in the midst of a major international disturbance involving Russia, Ukraine, Europe, and the United States. The disturbance began when Russia decided to not only invade Ukraine but annex the Crimean Peninsula as a part of Russia. This action came on the heels of major internal dissent in Ukraine concerning a national split over whether to move closer to Russia or closer to the countries of Europe. President Obama and America's European allies immediately imposed sanctions on Russia. The United Nations voted that the Russian invasion of Ukraine was illegal. Although the United States recognized the newly installed pro-Western government in Ukraine, the United States made it clear that America would not go to war over Ukraine.

Vatican City in Rome is home to the Catholic Church. It is also where the Pope, who is the religious leader of Catholics, resides. It was here also in March of 2014 that President Barack Obama met Pope Francis for the first time. This was not the first meeting between an American president and a Pope. Nevertheless, given the significant symbolism of the American presidency and the Catholic papacy, a meeting between an American president and the Catholic Pope is always considered historical. Although the meeting between Pope

Francis and President Obama was cordial, there stands a major area of disagreement between President Obama and the Pope over the use of contraceptives. The Catholic Church does not believe in contraception whereas President Obama sees it as a major component of women's health. On the other hand, a major area of agreement between Pope Francis and President Obama has to do with serving the poor and eradicating income inequality.

The year 2014, in addition to the disturbance in Ukraine, also began with major foreign policy setbacks in Iraq. In January the city of Fallujah fell to an Islamic militant force known as the Islamic State in Iraq and Syria (ISIS). In June, the city of Mosul was taken over. During the presidency of George W. Bush, these cities served as a gauge for what was called "The Surge." The Surge was a major military push by the United States that essentially turned the tides of the war in Iraq favorably toward the United States. Barack Obama, who was in the U.S. Senate at the time, had opposed the surge. As president, Obama admitted that the policy had been beneficial, and instituted a similar policy in Afghanistan. The troubling aspect surrounding the news of ISIS advances and large parts of Iraqi territory coming under their control stems from the fact that the United States had spent a great deal of money and lost a significant number of military lives in the war effort in Iraq. Iraqis suffered enormous losses as well.

The above three foreign policy scenarios are a small representation of the international reach of American foreign policy. These three events also illustrate how the president is both the chief diplomat and commander in chief of the Armed Forces, as discussed in Chapter Ten. Consequently, in addition to domestic policy, a major area of governing includes foreign policy. The president tends to take a major leadership role in the area of foreign policy. Modern expressions of American foreign policy began with Woodrow Wilson's involvement in World War I, Franklin Roosevelt's involvement in World War II, Truman's involvement in the Korean War, along with President Eisenhower's framework for the ensuing Cold War with the Soviet Union. Major military involvement subsequent to Eisenhower's framing of the Cold War include the Vietnam War, Ronald Reagan's support for "Freedom Fighters" in Nicaragua and Afghanistan, the wars in Iraq, Bill Clinton's air war in Serbia, and America's longest military engagement, the war in Afghanistan. This war began as "The War on Terror" shortly after the 9/11 attacks on the World Trade Center in New York City and the Pentagon in Washington, D.C.

There also exists in American foreign policy what is called an inherent "invitation to struggle" that exists between the president and Congress. Article I, Section 8 of the Constitution says that Congress has the power to "declare war." Article II of the Constitution says that the president shall be the commander in chief of the armed services. Two historical events are very exemplary of this "invitation to struggle" between the president and Congress. In 1964, Congress passed the Tonkin Gulf Resolution giving President Johnson unbridled authority to conduct the war in Southeast Asia as he saw fit. At the time, Senator Greening referred to the resolution as a "blank check." Shortly after passage of the resolution President Johnson presided over a massive build up of forces in Vietnam. This build up eventually led to the stationing of 500,000 troops in Vietnam. The war effort multiplied in cost and loss of life. This trend continued under President Nixon shortly after he was elected. Nixon expanded the war into Laos and Cambodia. President Nixon's action led Congress to pass the War Powers Resolution in 1973.

2. Joint Resolution of Congress H.J. RES 1145 August 7, 1964

Resolved by the Senate and House of Representatives of the United States of America in Congress assembled.

That the Congress approves and supports the determination of the President, as Commander in Chief, to take all necessary measures to repel any armed attack against the forces of the United States and to prevent further aggression.

Section 2. The United States regards as vital to its national interest and to world peace the maintenance of international peace and security in southeast Asia. Consonant with the Constitution of the United States and the Charter of the United Nations and in accordance with its obligations under the Southeast Asia Collective Defense Treaty, the United States is, therefore, prepared, as the President determines, to take all necessary steps, including the use of armed force, to assist any member or protocol state of the Southeast Asia Collective Defense Treaty requesting assistance in defense of its freedom.

Section 3. This resolution shall expire when the President shall determine that the peace and security of the area is reasonably assured by international conditions created by action of the United Nations or otherwise, except that it may be terminated earlier by concurrent resolution of the Congress. [1]

Figure 13-1

This presidential propensity for war without a declaration of war on the part of Congress led Congress to pass the War Powers Resolution in 1973. The purpose of the 1973 resolution was for Congress to regain its war making authority.

SEC. 4. (a) In the absence of a declaration of war, in any case in which United States Armed Forces are introduced—

(1) into hostilities or into situations where imminent involvement in hostilities is clearly indicated by the circumstances;
(2) into the territory, airspace or waters of a foreign nation, while equipped for combat, except for deployments which relate solely to supply, replacement, repair, or training of such forces; or
(3) in numbers which substantially enlarge United States Armed Forces equipped for combat already located in a foreign nation; the president shall submit within 48 hours to the Speaker of the House of Representatives and to the President pro tempore of the Senate a report, in writing, setting forth—
(A) the circumstances necessitating the introduction of United States Armed Forces;
(B) the constitutional and legislative authority under which such introduction took place; and
(C) the estimated scope and duration of the hostilities or involvement.

(b) The President shall provide such other information as the Congress may request in the fulfillment of its constitutional responsibilities with respect to committing the Nation to war and to the use of United States Armed Forces abroad

(c) Whenever United States Armed Forces are introduced into hostilities or into any situation described in subsection (a) of this section, the President shall, so long as such armed forces continue to be engaged in such hostilities or situation, report to the Congress periodically on the status of such hostilities or situation as well as on the scope and duration of such hostilities or situation, but in no event shall he report to the Congress less often than once every six months.

CONGRESSIONAL ACTION

SEC. 5. (a) Each report submitted pursuant to section 4(a)(1) shall be transmitted to the Speaker of the House of Representatives and to the President pro tempore of the Senate on the same calendar day. Each report so transmitted shall be referred to the Committee on Foreign Affairs of the House of Representatives and to the Committee on Foreign Relations of the Senate for appropriate action. If, when the report is transmitted, the Congress has adjourned sine die or has adjourned for any period in excess of three calendar days, the Speaker of the House of Representatives and the President pro tempore of the Senate, if they deem it advisable (or if petitioned by at least 30 percent of the membership of their respective Houses) shall jointly request the President to convene Congress in order that it may consider the report and take appropriate action pursuant to this section.

(b) Within sixty calendar days after a report is submitted or is required to be submitted pursuant to section 4(a)(1), whichever is earlier, the President shall terminate any use of United States Armed Forces with respect to which such report was submitted (or required to be submitted), unless the Congress (1) has declared war or has enacted a specific authorization for such use of United States Armed Forces, (2) has extended by law such sixty-day period, or (3) is physically unable to meet as a result of an armed attack upon the United

States. Such sixty-day period shall be extended for not more than an additional thirty days if the President determines and certifies to the Congress in writing that unavoidable military necessity respecting the safety of United States Armed Forces requires the continued use of such armed forces in the course of bringing about a prompt removal of such forces.

(c) Notwithstanding subsection (b), at any time that United States Armed Forces are engaged in hostilities outside the territory of the United States, its possessions and territories without a declaration of war or specific statutory authorization, such forces shall be removed by the President if the Congress so directs by concurrent resolution.[2]

2 Copyright in the Public Domain.

Figure 13-2

Section 4 begins with "in the absence of a declaration of war." This recognizes the constitutional authority of Congress to declare war while acknowledging the president as commander in chief of the Armed Services. Critics of the War Powers Resolution argue that the law gives the president at least a sixty-day window of war making authority that does not exist in the Constitution. What comes after the sixty-day window relates to congressional action. The specific action that Congress assigned to itself in such a situation has been referred to as a legislative veto. A legislative veto occurs when Congress or a committee of Congress orders executive action. The law states that the executive, after sixty days, must withdraw the troops from hostilities unless Congress declares war. It should be noted that the legislative veto was declared unconstitutional in the 1983 case INS v. Chadha.

Since Vietnam and the passage of the War Powers Resolution, there have been several uses of military force to carry out U.S. foreign objectives. On October 25, 1983 President Reagan ordered an invasion of the Caribbean island of Grenada. In 1989 President George H.W. Bush ordered the December invasion of Panama. These actions were taken without much congressional input. Nevertheless in other areas where the use of military force was applied, both Presidents Reagan and Bush worked with Congress on the use of military force. For example, ten years after the passage of the war powers resolution, the law was put to a severe test when President Reagan introduced American troops into Beirut, Lebanon in the face of significant congressional opposition. A compromise was reached with Congress. Although the War Powers Resolution authorized Congress to order the troops out after sixty days, Congress and Reagan agreed to allow the troops to remain at the air base in Lebanon for another ninety days. Shortly after the agreement was reached between the president and Congress, 240 Marines lost their lives when a truck bomber struck their compound at the airport in Beirut. After the bombing, Reagan ordered the troops out before the ninety day deadline expired. Presidents have increasingly sought congressional approval before committing American forces to areas of hostility. Examples of this include: authorization to use military force in the Iraq War (AUMF 1991), AUMF in Afghanistan 2001, and AUMF in Iraq 2002.

The 1991 authorization to use military force against Iraq was headed by George H. W. Bush. The war was based on Iraq's invasion of Kuwait. Based on old colonial realities, Iraq claimed that Kuwait was originally a part of Iraq before British colonialism. The American led United Nations action against Iraq was known as "Desert Storm." It was a brief war with a measured objective that maintained international support. This effort also helped the United States move a little more past its Vietnam Syndrome. The Vietnam Syndrome is the idea that each American military incursion could lead to a long term military involvement. Bill Clinton experienced this with a brief foray into Somalia. Wariness of the Vietnam Syndrome was also contributed to why the U.S. decision against introducing ground troops in its campaign against Serbia.

President Obama also proposed to ask Congress for an AUMF in Syria in 2013. This action came about after Syria crossed Obama's "redline," which involved the use of chemical weapons against its citizens. In August 2013, reports surfaced that Syria had used chemical weapons against its citizens. The Obama administration argued that military force was needed in order to nullify Syria's chemical arsenal. Republicans, who are normally "hawkish" on the use of military force, voiced skepticism about the president's push for military action in Syria. Realizing that a unilateral use of military force, without Congress signing on, could prove politically disastrous to the Obama presidency, the president stated that he would wait for Congress to vote on whether or not to use military force in Syria. Before Congress could vote on the resolution, Syria admitted to using chemical weapons and worked out an agreement with the United States and the world community to dismantle its chemical arsenal. Although war was avoided, the Syrian incident also reflected the inherent foreign policy struggle between Congress and the president.

Irrespective of the above incidents concerning AUMFs and the contexts of various wars, congressional declarations of war have only issued in five different wars:

Table 13.1

War of 1812 against the United Kingdom—June 18, 1812
Mexican-American War against Mexico—May 13, 1846
Spanish-American War against Spain—April 6, 1917
World War I against Austria-Hungary—December 7, 1917
World War II against Japan—December 8, 1941
Germany—December 11, 1941
Italy—June 5, 1942
Bulgaria
Hungary
Romania

One of America's most destructive wars was never declared by Congress. It was one of the first AUMF type authorizations for war. It was the Tonkin Gulf Resolution of 1964. The actual resolution was very brief; however, it was the basis of untold death and destruction (See Figure 13-1).

Some will argue that the war in Vietnam was a major event in the overall Cold War. The Cold War was an international geopolitical struggle between the United States and the Soviet Union. It was also characterized as a battle between capitalism and communism as well as a struggle between liberty and tyranny. The Cold War was initially framed as "containment." The idea of containment, which was adopted by the Eisenhower administration, was set forth in an article published in the journal *Foreign Affairs*. The idea of containment was to counter Soviet influence anywhere around the world either through the use of foreign aid or military force. The practice of containment directed American foreign policy all the way from President Eisenhower to Ronald Reagan. A subtext to containment was the nuclear arms race between the United States and the Soviet Union. This arms race was characterized by the idea of mutually assured destruction (MAD). MAD would be maintained by strike and counter strike capabilities.

The president has several advisors to assist in the formulation and implementation of foreign policy. The executive foreign policy apparatus first took official shape with the creation of the National Security Council in 1947. The security council was created by the National Security Act. The statutory members of the National Security Council include the President, the Vice President, the Secretary of State, the Secretary of Defense, and the National Security Advisor. Other members can be added at the president's discretion. From administration to administration the intelligence community is represented. Initially the Central Intelligence Agency coordinated America's intelligence collection. That responsibility now rests with the Office of National Intelligence. The intelligence community was a major actor in the Cold War. Eisenhower's first act of containment was on the continent of Africa in the Belgian Congo. When it was perceived that the newly elected Prime Minister Patrice Lumumba was leaning toward the Soviet Union, American intelligence was dispersed to the Belgian Congo in order to thwart Lumumba's efforts. Lumumba was assassinated by Belgian Congo forces on January 20, 1961. Eisenhower also had plans to end Fidel Castro's rule in Cuba. His plans, which included the Bay of Pigs invasion, were inherited by President Kennedy who did not offer expected air support for those who invaded Cuba. Containment was also at the forefront of President Reagan's unyielding support for apartheid in South Africa.

The congressional foreign policy apparatus is essentially located in the Senate. This apparatus is composed of congressional committees that assist Congress in carrying out its constitutional advice and consent function. These committees are the Senate Foreign Relations Committee and the Defense Committee. Discussions surrounding treaties and foreign policy appointments begin in the Senate Foreign Relations Committee. Issues surrounding the military or use of the military begin in the Senate Defense Committee.

The president of the United States is the chief diplomat of the United States. This role, by default, places the president as a major actor on the international stage. As a consequence, four presidents have been awarded the Nobel Peace Prize for their impact on global relations among nations. The first president to win the prize was Theodore Roosevelt. President Roosevelt was awarded the Prize for his efforts in ending the Russo-Japanese War. The next president to win the Nobel Prize for Peace was Woodrow Wilson. President Wilson won the prize for working to settle the Treaty of Versailles in ending World War I. The Treaty of Versailles also held the basis for the creation of the League of Nations. Wilson pushed very hard for the U.S. Senate to ratify the treaty but failed. This was a supreme irony that the American President was honored by the international community yet spurned the U.S. Senate. It has been stated that this rejection broke Wilson near the end of his presidency. Jimmy Carter was awarded the Nobel Prize; however, his award came several years after his presidency ended. President Carter was a one term president. He experienced many major setbacks in the area of foreign policy. In 1978 the United States lost a major East African ally in Ethiopia to the Soviet Union. Directly related to the missteps in the Horn of Africa was the Soviet invasion of Afghanistan in 1979. Although this invasion proved the undoing of the Soviet Union a decade later, at the time it made Carter seem weak in the international arena. The Carter administration also lost ground to the Soviets in Nicaragua and Grenada. The ultimate humiliation to President Carter came when the Shah of Iran, a staunch ally, was overthrown during the Iranian Revolution. During the revolution, the U.S. Embassy was overrun and several Americans were taken hostage. The hostage crisis in Iran consumed the last year of the Carter presidency and essentially paved the way for Ronald Reagan to be elected president in 1980. The Iranians did not release the hostages until after Reagan was sworn in as president. The irony of the Carter prize is that he was perceived as a weak president but rose to the level of international citizen post presidency. Working through the Carter Center, which is located in Atlanta, Georgia, Jimmy Carter has monitored elections worldwide and promoted numerous causes to uplift individuals in Africa, Asia, and Latin America. It was for these efforts that Carter was awarded the Noble Prize. The fourth American president to win a Nobel Peace Prize was Barack Obama. Both Obama and Reagan benefitted from a perceived inept foreign policy. Reagan was able to project an aura of strength as opposed to Carter's perceived weakness. President Obama won the Nobel Prize based on his emphasis on diplomacy as opposed to unilateral pushes for war. Ironically in his Nobel acceptance speech, President Obama stated that he is not opposed to all wars, only dumb wars. Obama stated that he believed in what he called "just" wars.

Table 13.2

AMERICAN PRESIDENTS AWARDED THE NOBEL PRIZE FOR PEACE	
1.	Theodore Roosevelt
2.	Woodrow Wilson
3.	Jimmy Carter
4.	Barack Obama

All U.S. presidents since Franklin Roosevelt have seemed obligated to use military force in some situation of international conflict. Roosevelt's entrance into World War II could possibly be seen as a just war in Obama's sense. Truman's use of the atomic bomb on Japan is more open to debate. Consequently, Obama became the first sitting U.S. president to win a Nobel Peace Prize since the advent of the modern presidency and Eisenhower's warning about the "military industrial complex." Although President Obama has not committed the United States to a new land war, his use of military drones has been quite controversial for essentially three reasons. First, there is the question of collateral damage regarding the death of innocent civilians. Second, the use of drones to kill suspected terrorists raises the question of summary executions. Third, where American citizens abroad have been involved, the question of due process is also raised.

Congressional involvement in the formulation and implementation of American foreign policy has generated considerable debate since the creation of the United States. As has been stated, the Constitution enumerates that the president is the commander in chief of America's armed forces. The Constitution also states that Congress has the power to declare war. This aspect of foreign policy tends to concern itself with military force. Yet, it must also be understood that Congress was given the power of advice and consent. This power comes through the Senate and is basically related to treaty ratification and appointee confirmation. As it relates to foreign policy, senatorial confirmation applies to a number of governmental positions. Some of these include: Secretary of State, Secretary of Defense, Ambassador to the United Nations, Director of Central Intelligence, Director of the Office of National Intelligence, all ambassadors to foreign countries, and the Chairman of the Joint Chiefs of Staff. Congressional input in U.S. foreign policy through confirmation varies according to the level of support that the nominee has in Congress. One of the more contentious appointees of late was Susan Rice, President Obama's former appointee as U.N. Ambassador. The fervor over Rice had to do with accusations that she assisted in a cover up regarding the U.S. consulate/embassy in Benghazi, Libya. President Obama pulled an end run around Congress and the controversy by appointing Rice as his National Security Advisor instead of fighting to place her as Secretary of State. The position of National Security Advisor is a high level foreign policy position that does not require senatorial confirmation. The National Security Advisor is considered to have only one constituent, the President of the United States.

A UNITED STATES DECLARATION OF INDEPENDENCE

In CONGRESS, July 4, 1776.
A DECLARATION
By the REPRESENTATIVES of the
UNITED STATES OF AMERICA,
In GENERAL CONGRESS assembled

WHEN in the course of human Events, it becomes necessary for one People to dissolve the Political Bands that have connected them with another, and to assume among the Powers of the Earth, the separate and equal Station to which the Laws of Nature and of Nature's God entitle them, a decent Respect to the Opinions of Mankind requires that they should declare the causes that impel them to the Separation.

We hold these Truths to be self-evident, that all Men are created equal, that they are endowed by their Creator with certain unalienable Rights, that among these are Life, Liberty, and the pursuit of Happiness—That to secure these Rights, Governments are instituted among Men, deriving their just Powers from the Consent of the Governed, that whenever any Form of Government becomes destructive of these Ends, it is the Right of the People to alter or abolish it, and to institute a new Government, laying its Foundation on such

Principles, and organizing its Powers in such Form, as to them shall seem most likely to effect their Safety and Happiness. Prudence, indeed, will dictate that Governments long established should not be changed for light and transient Causes; and accordingly all Experience hath shewn, that Mankind are more disposed to suffer, while Evils are sufferable, than to right themselves by abolishing the Forms to which they are accustomed. But when a long Train of abuses and usurpations, pursuing invariably the same object, evinces a Design to reduce them under absolute Despotism, it is their Right, it is their Duty, to throw off such Government, and to provide new Guards for their future Security. Such has been the patient Sufferance of these Colonies; and such is now the Necessity that constrains them to alter their former Systems of Government. The History of the Present King of Great-Britain is a History of repeated injuries and usurpations, all having in direct object the Establishment of an absolute Tyranny over these States. To prove this, let Facts be submitted to a candid World.

He has refused his assent to Laws, the most wholesome and necessary for the public Good.

He has forbidden his Governors to pass Laws of immediate and pressing importance, unless suspended in their operation till his assent should be obtained; and when so suspended, he has utterly neglected to attend to them.

He has refused to pass other Laws for the accommodation of large Districts of People; unless those People would relinquish the Right of Representation in the Legislature, a Right inestimable to them, and formidable to Tyrants only.

He has called together Legislative Bodies at Places unusual, uncomfortable, and distant from the Depository of their public Records, for the sole Purpose of fatiguing them into Compliance with his Measures.

He has dissolved Representative Houses repeatedly, for opposing with manly Firmness his invasions on the Rights of the People.

He has refused for a long Time, after such Dissolutions, to cause others to be elected; whereby the Legislative Powers, incapable of annihilation, have returned to the People at large for their exercise; the State remaining in the mean time exposed to all the Dangers of invasion from without, and Convulsions within.

He has endeavoured to prevent the Population of these States; for that Purpose obstructing the Laws for Naturalization of Foreigners; refusing to pass others to encourage their Migrations hither, and raising the Conditions of new appropriations of Lands.

He has obstructed the administration of Justice, by refusing his assent to Laws for establishing Judiciary Powers.

He has made Judges dependent on his Will alone, for the Tenure of their offices, and amount and Payment of their Salaries.

He has erected a Multitude of new offices, and sent hither Swarms of officers to harass our People, and eat out their Substance.

He has kept among us, in Times of Peace, Standing armies, without the consent of our Legislature.

He has affected to render the Military independent of and superior to the Civil Power.

He has combined with others to subject us to a Jurisdiction foreign to our Constitution, and unacknowledged by our Laws; giving his assent to their acts of pretended Legislation:

For quartering large Bodies of armed Troops among us:

For protecting them, by a mock Trial, from Punishment for any Murders which they should commit on the inhabitants of these States:

For cutting off our Trade with all Parts of the World:

For imposing taxes on us without our Consent:

For depriving us, in many Cases, of the Benefits of Trial by Jury:

For transporting us beyond Seas to be tried for pretended offences:

For abolishing the free System of English Laws in a neighbouring Province, establishing therein an arbitrary Government, and enlarging its Boundaries, so as to render it at once an Example and fit instrument for introducing the same absolute Rule in these Colonies:

For taking away our Charters, abolishing our most valuable Laws, and altering fundamentally the Forms of our Governments:

For suspending our own Legislatures, and declaring themselves invested with Powers to legislate for us in all Cases whatsoever.

He has abdicated Government here, by declaring us out of his Protection and waging War against us.

He has plundered our Seas, ravaged our Coasts, burnt our Towns, and destroyed the Lives of our People.

He is, at this Time, transporting large armies of foreign Mercenaries to compleat the Works of Death, Desolation, and Tyranny, already begun with circumstances of Cruelty and Perfidy, scarcely paralleled in the most barbarous ages, and totally unworthy the Head of a civilized Nation.

He has constrained our fellow Citizens taken Captive on the high Seas to bear arms against their Country, to become the Executioners of their Friends and Brethren, or to fall themselves by their Hands.

He has excited domestic insurrections among us, and has endeavoured to bring on the inhabitants of our Frontiers, the merciless indian Savages, whose known Rule of Warfare, is an undistinguished Destruction, of all ages, Sexes and Conditions.

In every stage of these oppressions we have Petitioned for Redress in the most humble Terms: our repeated Petitions have been answered only by repeated injury. a Prince, whose Character is thus marked by every act which may define a Tyrant, is unfit to be the Ruler of a free People.

Nor have we been wanting in attentions to our British Brethren. We have warned them from Time to Time of attempts by their Legislature to extend an unwarrantable Jurisdiction over us. We have reminded them of the Circumstances of our Emigration and Settlement here. We have appealed to their native Justice and Magnanimity, and we have conjured them by the Ties of our common Kindred to disavow these usurpations, which, would inevitably interrupt our Connections and Correspondence. They too have been deaf to the Voice of Justice and of Consanguinity. We must, therefore, acquiesce in the Necessity, which denounces our Separation, and hold them, as we hold the rest of Mankind, Enemies in War, in Peace, Friends.

We, therefore, the Representatives of the UNITED STATES OF AMERICA, in General Congress, assembled, appealing to the Supreme Judge of the World for the Rectitude of our intentions, do, in the Name, and by the authority of the good People of these Colonies, solemnly Publish and Declare, That these united Colonies are, and of Right ought to be, Free and independent States; that they are absolved from all allegiance to the British Crown, and that all political Connection between them and the State of Great-Britain, is and ought to be totally dissolved; and that as Free and Independent States, they have full Power to levy War, conclude Peace, contract alliances, establish Commerce, and to do all other acts and Things which Independent States may of right do. and for the support of this Declaration, with a firm Reliance on the Protection of the divine Providence, we mutually pledge to each other our Lives, our Fortunes, and our sacred Honor.

Signed by order and in Behalf of the Congress,
JOHN HANCOCK, President.

Attest.
CHARLES THOMSON, Secretary.

APPENDIX

B ARTICLES OF CONFEDERATION

To all to whom these Presents shall come,

We the undersigned Delegates of the States affixed to our Names send greeting:

Whereas the Delegates of the United States of America in Congress assembled did on the fifteenth day of November in the Year of our Lord One Thousand Seven Hundred and Seventy Seven, and in the Second Year of the Independence of America agree to certain articles of Confederation and perpetual Union between the States of New Hampshire, Massachusetts bay, Rhode Island and Providence Plantations, Connecticut, New York, New Jersey, Pennsylvania, Delaware, Maryland, Virginia, North Carolina, South Carolina and Georgia in the Words following, viz.

ARTICLES OF CONFEDERATION AND PERPETUAL UNION,

between the States of New Hampshire, Massachusetts bay, Rhode Island and Providence Plantations, Connecticut, New York, New Jersey, Pennsylvania, Delaware, Maryland, Virginia, North Carolina, South Carolina and Georgia.

Article. July 9, 1778. 1. The style of this confederacy shall be "The United States of America."

Art. 2. Each state retains its sovereignty, freedom, and independence, and every power, jurisdiction, and right, which is not by this confederation expressly delegated to the United States, in Congress assembled.

Art. 3. The said States hereby severally enter into a firm league of friendship with each other, for their common defense, the security of their liberties, and their mutual and general welfare, binding themselves to assist each other, against all force offered to, or attacks made upon them, or any of them, on account of religion, sovereignty, trade, or any other pretense whatever.

Art. 4. § 1. The better to secure and perpetuate mutual friendship and intercourse among the people of the different States in this Union, the free inhabitants of each of these States, paupers, vagabonds, and fugitives from justice excepted, shall be entitled to all privileges and immunities of free citizens in the several States; and the people of each State shall free ingress and regress to and from any other State, and shall enjoy therein all the privileges of trade and commerce, subject to the same duties, impositions, and restrictions as the inhabitants thereof respectively, provided that such restrictions shall not extend so far as to prevent the removal of property imported into any State, to any other State, of which the owner is an inhabitant; provided also that no imposition, duties or restriction shall be laid by any State, on the property of the United States, or either of them.

§ 2. If any person guilty of, or charged with, treason, felony, or other high misdemeanor in any State, shall flee from justice, and be found in any of the United States, he shall, upon demand of the governor or executive power of the State from which he fled, be delivered up and removed to the State having jurisdiction of his offense.

§ 3. Full faith and credit shall be given in each of these States to the records, acts, and judicial proceedings of the courts and magistrates of every other State.

Art. 5. § 1. For the most convenient management of the general interests of the United States, delegates shall be annually appointed in such manner as the legislatures of each State shall direct, to meet in Congress on the first Monday in November, in every year, with a power reserved to each State to recall its delegates, or any of them, at any time within the year, and to send others in their stead for the remainder of the year. July 9, 1778. § 2. No State shall be represented in Congress by less than two, nor more than seven members; and no person shall be capable of being a delegate for more than three years in any term of six years; nor shall any person, being a delegate, be capable of holding any office under the United States, for which he, or another for his benefit, receives any salary, fees or emolument of any kind.

§ 3. Each State shall maintain its own delegates in a meeting of the States, and while they act as members of the committee of the States.

§ 4. In determining questions in the United States in Congress assembled, each State shall have one vote.

§ 5. Freedom of speech and debate in Congresshall not be impeached or questioned in any court or place out of Congress, and the members of Congresshall be protected in their persons from arrests or imprisonments, during the time of their going to and from, and attendance on Congress, except for treason, felony, or breach of the peace.

Art. 6. § 1. No State, without the consent of the United States in Congress assembled, shall send any embassy to, or receive any embassy from, or enter into any conference, agreement, alliance or treaty with any King, Prince or State; nor shall any person holding any office of profit or trust under the United States, or any of them, accept any present, emolument, office or title of any kind whatever from any King, Prince or foreign State; nor shall the United States in Congress assembled, or any of them, grant any title of nobility.

§ 2. No two or more States shall enter into any treaty, confederation or alliance whatever between them, without the consent of the United

States in Congress assembled, specifying accurately the purposes for which the same is to be entered into, and how long it shall continue.

§ 3. No State shall lay any imposts or duties, which may interfere with any stipulations in treaties, entered into by the United States in Congress assembled, with any King, Prince or State, in pursuance of any treaties already proposed by Congress, to the courts of France and Spain.

§ 4. No vessel of war shall be kept up in time of peace by any State, except such number only, as shall be deemed necessary by the United States in Congress assembled, for the defense of such State, or its trade; nor shall any body of forces be kept up by any State in time of peace, except such number only, as in the judgement of the United States in Congress assembled, shall be deemed requisite to garrison the forts necessary for the defense of such State; but every State shall always keep up a well-regulated and disciplined militia, sufficiently armed and accoutered, and shall provide and constantly have ready for use, in public stores, a due number of filed pieces and tents, and a proper quantity of arms, ammunition and camp equipage.

§ 5. No State shall engage in any war without the consent of the United States in Congress assembled, unless such State be actually invaded by enemies, or shall have received certain advice of a resolution being formed by some nation of Indians to invade such State, and the danger is so imminent as not to admit of a delay till the United States in Congress assembled can be consulted; nor shall any State grant commissions to any ships or vessels of war, nor letters of marque or reprisal, except it be after a declaration of war by the United States in Congress assembled, and then only against the Kingdom or State and the subjects thereof, against which war has been so declared, and under such regulations as shall be established by the United States in Congress assembled, unless such State be infested by pirates, in which case vessels of war may be fitted out for that occasion, and kept so long as the danger shall continue, or until the United States in Congress assembled shall determine otherwise.

July 9, 1778. Art. 7. When land forces are raised by any State for the common defense, all officers of or under the rank of colonel, shall be appointed by the legislature of each State respectively, by whom such forces shall be raised, or in such manner as such State shall direct, and all vacancies shall be filled up by the State which first made the appointment.

Art. 8. All charges of war, and all other expenses that shall be incurred for the common defense or general welfare, and allowed by the United States in Congress assembled, shall be defrayed out of a common treasury, which shall be supplied by the several States in proportion to the value of all land within each State, granted or surveyed for any person, as such land and the buildings and improvements thereon shall be estimated according to such mode as the United States in Congress assembled, shall from time to time direct and appoint. The taxes for paying that proportion shall be laid and levied by the authority and direction of the legislatures of the several States within the time agreed upon by the United States in Congress assembled.

Art. 9. § 1. The United States in Congress assembled, shall have the sole and exclusive right and power of determining on peace and war, except in the cases mentioned in the sixth Article, of sending and receiving ambassadors; entering into treaties and alliances, provided that no treaty of commerce shall be made whereby the legislative power of the respective States shall be restrained from imposing such imposts and duties on foreigners, as their own people are subjected to, or from prohibiting the exportation or importation of any species of goods or commodities whatsoever; of establishing rules for deciding in all cases, what captures on land or water shall be legal, and in what manner prizes taken by land or naval forces in the service of the United States shall be divided or appropriated; of granting letters of marque and reprisal in times of peace; appointing courts for the trial of piracies and felonies committed on the high seas and establishing courts for receiving and determining finally appeals in all cases of captures, provided that no member of Congress shall be appointed a judge of any of the said courts.

§ 2. The United States in Congress assembled shall also be the last resort on appeal in all disputes and differences now subsisting or that hereafter may arise between two or more States concerning boundary, jurisdiction or any other causes whatever; which authority shall always be exercised in the manner following. Whenever the legislative or executive authority or lawful agent of any State in controversy with another shall present a petition to Congress stating the matter in question and praying for a hearing, notice thereof shall be given by order of Congress to the legislative or executive authority of the other State in controversy, and a day assigned for the appearance of the parties by their lawful agents, who shall then be directed to appoint by joint consent, commissioners or judges to constitute a court for hearing and determining the matter in question: but if they cannot agree, Congress shall name three persons out of each of the United States, and from the list of such persons each party shall alternately strike out one, the petitioners beginning, until the number shall be reduced to thirteen; and from that number not less than seven, nor more than nine names as Congress shall direct, shall in the presence of Congress be drawn out by lot, and the persons whose names shall be so drawn or any five of them, shall be commissioners or judges, to hear and finally determine the controversy, so always as a major part of the judges who shall hear the cause shall agree in the determination: and if either party shall neglect to attend at the day appointed, without showing reasons, which Congress shall judge sufficient, or being present shall refuse to strike, the Congress shall proceed to nominate three persons out of each State, and the secretary of Congress shall strike in behalf of such party absent July 9, 1778. or refusing; and the judgement and sentence of the court to be appointed, in the manner before prescribed, shall be final and conclusive; and if any of the parties shall refuse to submit to the authority of such court, or to appear or defend their claim or cause, the court shall nevertheless proceed to pronounce sentence, or judgement, which shall in like manner be final and decisive, the judgement or sentence and other proceedings being in either case transmitted to Congress, and lodged among the acts of Congress for the security of the parties concerned; provided that every commissioner, before he sits in judgement, shall take an oath to be administered by one of the judges of the supreme or superior court of the State, where the cause shall be tried, "well and truly to hear and determine the matter in question, according to the best of his judgement, without favor, affection or hope of reward." Provided, also, that no State shall be deprived of territory for the benefit of the United States.

§ 3. All controversies concerning the private right of soil claimed under different grants of two or more States, whose jurisdictions as they may respect such lands, and the States which passed such grants are adjusted, the said grants or either of them being at the same time claimed to have originated antecedent to such settlement of jurisdiction, shall on the petition of either party to the Congress of the United States, be finally determined as near as may be in the same manner as is before prescribed for deciding disputes respecting territorial jurisdiction between different States.

§ 4. The United States in Congress assembled shall also have the sole and exclusive right and power of regulating the alloy and value of coin struck by their own authority, or by that of the respective States; fixing the standards of weights and measures throughout the United States; regulating the trade and managing all affairs with the Indians, not members of any of the States, provided that the legislative right of any State within its own limits be not infringed or violated; establishing or regulating post offices from one State to another, throughout all the United States, and exacting such postage on the papers passing through the same as may be requisite to defray the expenses of the said office; appointing all officers of the land forces, in the service of the United States, excepting regimental officers; appointing all the officers of the naval forces, and commissioning all officers whatever in the service of the United States; making rules for the government and regulation of the said land and naval forces, and directing their operations.

§ 5. The United States in Congress assembled shall have authority to appoint a committee, to sit in the recess of Congress, to be denominated, *"A Committee of the States,"* and to consist of one delegate from each State; and to appoint such other committees and civil officers as may be necessary for managing the general affairs of the United States under their direction; to appoint one of their members to preside, provided that no person be allowed to serve in the office of president more than one year in any term of three years; to ascertain the necessary sums of money to be raised for the service of the United States, and to appropriate and apply the same for defraying the public expenses; to borrow money, or emit bills on the credit of the United States, transmitting every half-year to the respective States an account of the sums of money so borrowed or emitted; to build and equip a navy; to agree upon the number of land forces, and to make requisitions from each State for its quota, in proportion to the number of white inhabitants in such State; which requisition shall be binding, and thereupon the legislature of each State shall appoint the regimental officers, raise the men and clothe, arm and equip them in a soldier-like manner, at the expense of the United States; and the officers and men so clothed, armed and equipped shall march to the place appointed, and within July 9, 1778. the time agreed on by the United States in Congress assembled. But if the United States in Congress assembled shall, on consideration of circumstances judge proper that any State should not raise men, or should raise a smaller number of men than the quota thereof, such extra number shall be raised, officered, clothed, armed and equipped in the same manner as the quota of each State, unless the legislature of such State shall judge that such extra number cannot be safely spread out in the same, in which case they shall raise, officer, clothe, arm and equip as many of such extra number as they judge can be safely spared. And the officers and men so clothed, armed, and equipped, shall march to the place appointed, and within the time agreed on by the United States in Congress assembled.

§ 6. The United States in Congress assembled shall never engage in a war, nor grant letters of marque or reprisal in time of peace, nor enter into any treaties or alliances, nor coin money, nor regulate the value thereof, nor ascertain the sums and expenses necessary for the defense and welfare of the United States, or any of them, nor emit bills, nor borrow money on the credit of the United States, nor appropriate money, nor agree upon the number of vessels of war, to be built or purchased, or the number of land or sea forces to be raised, nor appoint a commander in chief of the army or navy, unless nine States assent to the same: nor shall a question on any other point, except for adjourning from day to day be determined, unless by the votes of the majority of the United States in Congress assembled.

§ 7. The Congress of the United States shall have power to adjourn to any time within the year, and to any place within the United States, so that no period of adjournment be for a longer duration than the space of six months, and shall publish the journal of their proceedings monthly, except such parts thereof relating to treaties, alliances or military operations, as in their judgement require secrecy; and the yeas and nays of the delegates of each State on any question shall be entered on the journal, when it is desired by any delegates of a State, or any of them, at his or their request shall be furnished with a transcript of the said journal, except such parts as are above excepted, to lay before the legislatures of the several States.

Art. 10. The Committee of the States, or any nine of them, shall be authorized to execute, in the recess of Congress, such of the powers of Congress as the United States in Congress assembled, by the consent of the nine States, shall from time to time think expedient to vest them with; provided that no power be delegated to the said Committee, for the exercise of which, by the Articles of Confederation, the voice of nine States in the Congress of the United States assembled be requisite.

Art. 11. Canada acceding to this confederation, and adjoining in the measures of the United States, shall be admitted into, and entitled to all the advantages of this Union; but no other colony shall be admitted into the same, unless such admission be agreed to by nine States.

Art. 12. All bills of credit emitted, monies borrowed, and debts contracted by, or under the authority of Congress, before the assembling of the United States, in pursuance of the present confederation, shall be deemed and considered as a charge against the United States, for payment and satisfaction whereof the said United States, and the public faith are hereby solemnly pledged.

Art. 13. Every State shall abide by the determination of the United States in Congress assembled, on all questions which by this confederation are submitted to them. And the Articles of this Confederation shall be inviolably observed by every State, and the Union shall be perpetual; nor shall any alteration at any time hereafter be made in any of them; unless such alteration be agreed to in a Congress of the July 9, 1778. United States, and be afterwards confirmed by the legislatures of every State.

And whereas it hath pleased the great Governor of the world to incline the hearts of the legislatures we respectively represent in Congress, to approve of, and to authorize us to ratify the said articles of confederation and perpetual union, Know ye, that we, the undersigned delegates, by virtue of the power and authority to us given for that purpose, do, by these presents, in the name and in behalf of our respective constituents, fully and entirely ratify and confirm each and every of the said articles of confederation and perpetual union, and all and singular the matters and things therein contained. And we do further solemnly plight and engage the faith of our respective constituents, that they shall abide by the determinations of the United States, in Congress assembled, on all questions which by the said confederation are submitted to them; and that the articles thereof shall be inviolably observed by the States we respectively represent, and that the Union shall be perpetual. In witness whereof, we have hereunto set our hands, in Congress.

Done at Philadelphia, in the State of Pennsylvania, the 9th day of July, in the Year of our Lord 1778, and in the third year of the Independence of America.

On the part and behalf of the State of New Hampshire.—Josiah Bartlett, John Wentworth Jun. (August 8, 1778.)

On the part and behalf of The State of Massachusetts Bay.—John Hancock, Francis Dana, Samuel Adams, James Lovell, Elbridge Gerry, Samuel Holten

On the part and behalf of the State of Rhode Island and Providence Plantations.—William Ellery, John Collins, Henry Marchant

On the part and behalf of the State of Connecticut.—Roger Sherman, Titus Hosmer, Samuel Huntington, Andrew Adams, Oliver Wolcott

On the part and behalf of the State of New York.—James Duane, Wm Duer, Francis Lewis, Gouv Morris

On the part and in behalf of the State of New Jersey.—Jno. Witherspoon, Nath. Scudder, (November 26, 1778.)

On the part and behalf of the State of Pennsylvania.—Robert Morris, Daniel Roberdeau, Jona. Bayard Smith, William Clingan, Joseph Reed, (July 22, 1778.)

On the part and behalf of the State of Delaware.—Thomas M'Kean, (February 12, 1779,) John Dickinson, (May 5, 1779,) Nicholas Van Dyke.

On the part and behalf of the State of Maryland.—John Hanson, (March 1, 1781,) Daniel Carroll, (March 1, 1781.)

On the part and behalf of the State of Virginia.—Richard Henry Lee, John Banister, Thomas Adams, Jno. Harvie, Francis Lightfoot Lee.

On the part and behalf of the State of North Carolina.—John Penn, (July 21 1778,) Corns. Harnett, Jno. Williams.

On the part and behalf of the State of South Carolina.—Henry Laurens, William Henry Drayton, Jno. Mathews, Richard Hutson, Thos. Heyward, Jun.

On the part and behalf of the State of Georgia.—Jno. Walton, (July 24, 1778,) Edwd. Telfair, Edward Langworthy.

APPENDIX

C CONSTITUTION OF THE UNITED STATES OF AMERICA

We the People of the United States, in order to form a more perfect union, establish Justice, insure domestic Tranquility, provide for the common defence, promote the general Welfare, and secure the Blessings of Liberty to ourselves and our Posterity, do ordain and establish this Constitution for the united States of america.

Article I

Section 1

All legislative Powers herein granted shall be vested in a Congress of the united States, which shall consist of a Senate and House of Representatives.

Section 2

The House of Representatives shall be composed of Members chosen every second year by the People of the several States, and the Electors in each State shall have the Qualifications requisite for Electors of the most numerous Branch of the State Legislature.

No Person shall be a Representative who shall not have attained to the age of twenty five years, and been seven years a Citizen of the united States, and who shall not, when elected, be an inhabitant of that State in which he shall be chosen.

Representatives and direct Taxes shall be apportioned among the several States which may be included within this union, according to their respective Numbers, which shall be determined by adding to the whole Number of free Persons, including those bound to Service for a Term of years, and excluding indians not taxed, three fifths of all other Persons. The actual Enumeration shall be made within three years after the first Meeting of the Congress of the united States, and within every subsequent Term of ten years, in such Manner as they shall by Law direct. The Number of Representatives shall not exceed one for every thirty Thousand, but each State shall have at Least one Representative; and until such enumeration shall be made, the State of New Hampshire shall be entitled to chuse three, Massachusetts eight, Rhode-Island and Providence Plantations one, Connecticut five, New-York six, New Jersey four, Pennsylvania eight, Delaware one, Maryland six, Virginia ten, North Carolina five, South Carolina five, and Georgia three.

When vacancies happen in the Representation from any State, the Executive authority thereof shall issue Writs of Election to fill such Vacancies.

The House of Representatives shall chuse their Speaker and other officers; and shall have the sole Power of impeachment.

Section 3

The Senate of the united States shall be composed of two Senators from each State, chosen by the Legislature thereof, for six years; and each Senator shall have one Vote.

Immediately after they shall be assembled in Consequence of the first Election, they shall be divided as equally as may be into three Classes. The Seats of the Senators of the first Class shall be vacated at the

Expiration of the second year, of the second Class at the Expiration of the fourth year, and of the third Class at the Expiration of the sixth year, so that one third may be chosen every second year; and if Vacancies happen by Resignation, or otherwise, during the Recess of the Legislature of any State, the Executive thereof may make temporary appointments until the next Meeting of the Legislature, which shall then fill such Vacancies.

No Person shall be a Senator who shall not have attained to the age of thirty years, and been nine years a Citizen of the united States, and who shall not, when elected, be an inhabitant of that State for which he shall be chosen.

The Vice President of the united States shall be President of the Senate but shall have no Vote, unless they be equally divided.

The Senate shall chuse their other officers, and also a President pro tempore, in the absence of the Vice President, or when he shall exercise the office of President of the united States.

The Senate shall have the sole Power to try all impeachments. When sitting for that Purpose, they shall be on oath or affirmation. When the President of the united States is tried the Chief Justice shall preside: and no Person shall be convicted without the Concurrence of two thirds of the Members present.

Judgment in Cases of impeachment shall not extend further than to removal from office, and disqualification to hold and enjoy any office of honor, Trust or Profit under the united States: but the Party convicted shall nevertheless be liable and subject to indictment, Trial, Judgment and Punishment, according to Law.

Section 4

The Times, Places and Manner of holding Elections for Senators and Representatives, shall be prescribed in each State by the Legislature thereof; but the Congress may at any time by Law make or alter such Regulations, except as to the Places of chusing Senators.

The Congress shall assemble at least once in every year, and such Meeting shall be on the first Monday in December, unless they shall by Law appoint a different Day.

Section 5

Each House shall be the Judge of the Elections, Returns and Qualifications of its own Members, and a Majority of each shall constitute a Quorum to do Business; but a smaller Number may adjourn from day to day, and may be authorized to compel the attendance of absent Members, in such Manner, and under such Penalties as each House may provide.

Each House may determine the Rules of its Proceedings, punish its Members for disorderly Behaviour, and, with the Concurrence of two thirds, expel a Member.

Each House shall keep a Journal of its Proceedings, and from time to time publish the same, excepting such Parts as may in their Judgment require Secrecy; and the yeas and Nays of the Members of either House on any question shall, at the Desire of one fifth of those Present, be entered on the Journal.

Neither House, during the Session of Congress, shall, without the Consent of the other, adjourn for more than three days, nor to any other Place than that in which the two Houses shall be sitting.

Section 6

The Senators and Representatives shall receive a Compensation for their Services, to be ascertained by Law, and paid out of the Treasury of the united States. They shall in all Cases, except Treason, Felony and Breach of the Peace, be privileged from arrest during their attendance at the Session of their respective Houses, and in going to and returning from the same; and for any Speech or Debate in either House, they shall not be questioned in any other Place.

No Senator or Representative shall, during the Time for which he was elected, be appointed to any civil office under the authority of the united States, which shall have been created, or the Emoluments whereof shall have been encreased during such time; and no Person holding any office under the united States, shall be a Member of either House during his Continuance in office.

Section 7

All Bills for raising Revenue shall originate in the House of Representatives; but the Senate may propose or concur with amendments as on other Bills.

Every Bill which shall have passed the House of Representatives and the Senate, shall, before it become a law, be presented to the President of the united States: if he approve he shall sign it, but if not he shall return it, with his objections to that House in which it shall have originated, who shall enter the objections at large on their Journal, and proceed to reconsider it. if after such Reconsideration two thirds of that House shall agree to pass the Bill, it shall be sent, together with the objections, to the other House, by which it shall likewise be reconsidered, and if approved by two thirds of that House, it shall become a Law. But in all such Cases the Votes of both Houses shall be determined by yeas and Nays, and the Names of the Persons voting for and against the Bill shall be entered on the Journal of each House respectively. if any Bill shall not be returned by the President within ten Days (Sundays excepted) after it shall have been presented to him, the Same shall be a Law, in like Manner as if he had signed it, unless the Congress by their adjournment prevent its Return, in which Case it shall not be a Law.

Every order, Resolution, or Vote to which the Concurrence of the Senate and House of Representatives may be necessary (except on a question of adjournment) shall be presented to the President of the united States; and before the Same shall take Effect, shall be approved by him, or being disapproved by him, shall be repassed by two thirds of the Senate and House of Representatives, according to the Rules and Limitations prescribed in the Case of a Bill.

Section 8

The Congress shall have Power To lay and collect Taxes, Duties, imposts and Excises, to pay the Debts and provide for the common Defence and general Welfare of the united States; but all Duties, imposts and Excises shall be uniform throughout the united States;

To borrow Money on the credit of the united States;

To regulate Commerce with foreign Nations, and among the several States, and with the indian Tribes;

To establish an uniform Rule of Naturalization, and uniform Laws on the subject of Bankruptcies throughout the united States;

To coin Money, regulate the Value thereof, and of foreign Coin, and fix the Standard of Weights and Measures;

To provide for the Punishment of counterfeiting the Securities and current Coin of the united States;

To establish Post offices and post Roads;

To promote the Progress of Science and useful arts, by securing for limited Times to authors and inventors the exclusive Right to their respective Writings and Discoveries;

To constitute Tribunals inferior to the supreme Court;

To define and punish Piracies and Felonies committed on the high Seas, and offences against the Law of Nations;

To declare War, grant Letters of Marque and Reprisal, and make Rules concerning Captures on Land and Water;

To raise and support armies, but no appropriation of Money to that use shall be for a longer Term than two years;

To provide and maintain a Navy;

To make Rules for the Government and Regulation of the land and naval Forces;

To provide for calling forth the Militia to execute the Laws of the union, suppress insurrections and repel invasions;

To provide for organizing, arming, and disciplining, the Militia, and for governing such Part of them as may be employed in the Service of the united States, reserving to the States respectively, the appointment of the officers, and the authority of training the Militia according to the discipline prescribed by Congress;

To exercise exclusive Legislation in all Cases whatsoever, over such District (not exceeding ten Miles square) as may, by Cession of Particular States, and the acceptance of Congress, become the Seat of the Government of the united States, and to exercise like authority over all Places purchased by the Consent of the Legislature of the State in which the Same shall be, for the Erection of Forts, Magazines, arsenals, dock-Yards and other needful Buildings;—And

To make all Laws which shall be necessary and proper for carrying into Execution the foregoing Powers and all other Powers vested by this Constitution in the Government of the united States, or in any Department or officer thereof.

Section 9

The Migration or importation of such Persons as any of the States now existing shall think proper to admit, shall not be prohibited by the

Congress prior to the year one thousand eight hundred and eight, but a Tax or duty may be imposed on such importation, not exceeding ten dollars for each Person.

The Privilege of the Writ of Habeas Corpus shall not be suspended, unless when in Cases of Rebellion or invasion the public Safety may require it.

No Bill of attainder or ex post facto Law shall be passed.

No Capitation, or other direct, Tax shall be laid, unless in Proportion to the Census or Enumeration herein before directed to be taken.

No Tax or Duty shall be laid on articles exported from any State.

No Preference shall be given by any Regulation of Commerce or Revenue to the Ports of one State over those of another: nor shall Vessels bound to, or from, one State, be obliged to enter, clear or pay Duties in another.

No Money shall be drawn from the Treasury, but in Consequence of appropriations made by Law; and a regular Statement and account of the Receipts and Expenditures of all public Money shall be published from time to time.

No Title of Nobility shall be granted by the united States: and no Person holding any office of Profit or Trust under them, shall, without the Consent of the Congress, accept of any present, Emolument, office, or Title, of any kind whatever, from any King, Prince or foreign State.

Section 10

No State shall enter into any Treaty, alliance, or Confederation; grant Letters of Marque and Reprisal; coin Money; emit Bills of Credit; make any Thing but gold and silver Coin a Tender in Payment of Debts; pass any Bill of attainder, ex post facto Law, or Law impairing the obligation of Contracts, or grant any Title of Nobility.

No State shall, without the Consent of the Congress, lay any imposts or Duties on imports or Exports, except what may be absolutely necessary for executing it's inspection Laws: and the net Produce of all Duties and imposts, laid by any State on imports or Exports, shall be for the use of the Treasury of the united States; and all such Laws shall be subject to the Revision and Controul of the Congress.

No State shall, without the Consent of Congress, lay any Duty of Tonnage, keep Troops, or Ships of War in time of Peace, enter into any agreement or Compact with another State, or with a foreign Power, or engage in War, unless actually invaded, or in such imminent Danger as will not admit of delay.

Article II

Section 1

The executive Power shall be vested in a President of the united States of america. He shall hold his office during the Term of four years, and, together with the Vice President, chosen for the same Term, be elected, as follows:

Each State shall appoint, in such Manner as the Legislature thereof may direct, a Number of Electors, equal to the whole Number of Senators and Representatives to which the State may be entitled in the Congress: but no Senator or Representative, or Person holding an office of Trust or Profit under the united States, shall be appointed an Elector.

The Electors shall meet in their respective States, and vote by Ballot for two Persons, of whom one at least shall not be an inhabitant of the same State with themselves. and they shall make a List of all the Persons voted for, and of the Number of Votes for each; which List they shall sign and certify, and transmit sealed to the Seat of the Government of the united States, directed to the President of the Senate. The President of the Senate shall, in the Presence of the Senate and House of Representatives, open all the Certificates, and the Votes shall then be counted. The Person having the greatest Number of Votes shall be the President, if such Number be a Majority of the whole Number of Electors appointed; and if there be more than one who have such Majority, and have an equal Number of Votes, then the House of Representatives shall immediately chuse by Ballot one of them for President; and if no Person have a Majority, then from the five highest on the List the said House shall in like Manner chuse the President. But in chusing the President, the Votes shall be taken by States, the Representatives from each State having one Vote; a quorum for this Purpose shall consist of a Member or Members from two thirds of the States, and a Majority of all the States shall be necessary to a Choice. in every Case, after the Choice of the President, the Person having the greatest Number of Votes of the Electors shall be the Vice President. But if there should remain two or more who have equal Votes, the Senate shall chuse from them by Ballot the Vice President.

The Congress may determine the Time of chusing the Electors, and the Day on which they shall give their Votes; which Day shall be the same throughout the united States.

No Person except a natural born Citizen, or a Citizen of the united States, at the time of the adoption of this Constitution, shall be eligible to the office of President; neither shall any person be eligible to that office who shall not have attained to the age of thirty five years, and been fourteen years a Resident within the united States.

In Case of the Removal of the President from office, or of his Death, Resignation, or inability to discharge the Powers and Duties of the said office, the Same shall devolve on the Vice President, and the Congress may by Law provide for the Case of Removal, Death, Resignation or inability, both of the President and Vice President, declaring what officer shall then act as President, and such officer shall act accordingly, until the Disability be removed, or a President shall be elected.

The President shall, at stated Times, receive for his Services, a Compensation, which shall neither be encreased nor diminished during the Period for which he shall have been elected, and he shall not receive within that Period any other Emolument from the united States, or any of them.

Before he enter on the Execution of his office, he shall take the following oath or affirmation:—"I do solemnly swear (or affirm) that I will faithfully execute the office of President of the united States, and will to the best of my ability, preserve, protect and defend the Constitution of the united States."

Section 2

The President shall be Commander in Chief of the army and Navy of the united States, and of the Militia of the several States, when called into the actual Service of the united States; he may require the opinion, in writing, of the principal officer in each of the executive Departments, upon any Subject relating to the Duties of their respective offices, and he shall have Power to Grant Reprieves and Pardons for offences against the united States, except in Cases of impeachment.

He shall have Power, by and with the advice and Consent of the Senate, to make Treaties, provided two thirds of the Senators present concur; and he shall nominate, and by and with the advice and Consent of the Senate, shall appoint ambassadors, other public Ministers and Consuls, Judges of the supreme Court, and all other officers of the united States, whose appointments are not herein otherwise provided for, and which shall be established by Law: but the Congress may by Law vest the appointment of such inferior officers, as they think proper, in the President alone, in the Courts of Law, or in the Heads of Departments.

The President shall have Power to fill up all Vacancies that may happen during the Recess of the Senate, by granting Commissions which shall expire at the End of their next Session.

Section 3

He shall from time to time give to the Congress information on the State of the union, and recommend to their Consideration such Measures as he shall judge necessary and expedient; he may, on extraordinary occasions, convene both Houses, or either of them, and in Case of Disagreement between them, with Respect to the Time of adjournment, he may adjourn them to such Time as he shall think proper; he shall receive ambassadors and other public Ministers; he shall take Care that the Laws be faithfully executed, and shall Commission all the officers of the united States.

Section 4

The President, Vice President and all Civil officers of the united States, shall be removed from office on impeachment for and Conviction of, Treason, Bribery, or other high Crimes and Misdemeanors.

Article. III

Section 1

The judicial Power of the united States, shall be vested in one supreme Court, and in such inferior Courts as the Congress may from time to time ordain and establish. The Judges, both of the supreme and inferior Courts, shall hold their offices during good Behaviour, and shall, at stated Times, receive for their Services, a Compensation, which shall not be diminished during their Continuance in office.

Section 2

The judicial Power shall extend to all Cases, in Law and Equity, arising under this Constitution, the Laws of the united States, and Treaties made, or which shall be made, under their authority;—to all Cases affecting ambassadors, other public ministers and Consuls;—to all Cases of admiralty and maritime Jurisdiction;—to Controversies to which the united States shall be a Party;—to Controversies between two or more States;—between a State and Citizens of another State;—between Citizens of different States;—between Citizens of the same

State claiming Lands under Grants of different States, and between a State, or the Citizens thereof, and foreign States, Citizens or Subjects.

In all Cases affecting ambassadors, other public Ministers and Consuls, and those in which a State shall be Party, the supreme Court shall have original Jurisdiction. in all the other Cases before mentioned, the supreme Court shall have appellate Jurisdiction, both as to Law and Fact, with such Exceptions, and under such Regulations as the Congress shall make.

The Trial of all Crimes, except in Cases of impeachment, shall be by Jury; and such Trial shall be held in the State where the said Crimes shall have been committed; but when not committed within any State, the Trial shall be at such Place or Places as the Congress may by Law have directed.

Section 3

Treason against the united States, shall consist only in levying War against them, or in adhering to their Enemies, giving them aid and Comfort. No Person shall be convicted of Treason unless on the Testimony of two Witnesses to the same overt act, or on Confession in open Court.

The Congress shall have Power to declare the Punishment of Treason, but no attainder of Treason shall work Corruption of Blood, or Forfeiture except during the Life of the Person attainted.

Article IV

Section 1

Full Faith and Credit shall be given in each State to the public acts, Records, and judicial Proceedings of every other State. and the Congress may by general Laws prescribe the Manner in which such acts, Records and Proceedings shall be proved, and the Effect thereof.

Section 2

The Citizens of each State shall be entitled to all Privileges and immunities of Citizens in the several States.

A Person charged in any State with Treason, Felony, or other Crime, who shall flee from Justice, and be found in another State, shall on Demand of the executive authority of the State from which he fled, be delivered up, to be removed to the State having Jurisdiction of the Crime.

No Person held to Service or Labour in one State, under the Laws thereof, escaping into another, shall, in Consequence of any Law or Regulation therein, be discharged from such Service or Labour, but shall be delivered up on Claim of the Party to whom such Service or Labour may be due.

Section 3

New States may be admitted by the Congress into this union; but no new State shall be formed or erected within the Jurisdiction of any other State; nor any State be formed by the Junction of two or more States, or Parts of States, without the Consent of the Legislatures of the States concerned as well as of the Congress.

The Congress shall have Power to dispose of and make all needful Rules and Regulations respecting the Territory or other Property belonging to the united States; and nothing in this Constitution shall be so construed as to Prejudice any Claims of the united States, or of any particular State.

Section 4

The united States shall guarantee to every State in this union a Republican Form of Government, and shall protect each of them against invasion; and on application of the Legislature, or of the Executive (when the Legislature cannot be convened) against domestic Violence.

Article V

The Congress, whenever two thirds of both Houses shall deem it necessary, shall propose amendments to this Constitution, or, on the application of the Legislatures of two thirds of the several States, shall call a Convention for proposing amendments, which, in either Case, shall be valid to all intents and Purposes, as Part of this Constitution, when ratified by the Legislatures of three fourths of the several States, or by Conventions in three fourths thereof, as the one or the other Mode of Ratification may be proposed by the Congress; Provided that no amendment which may be made prior to the year one thousand eight hundred and eight shall in any Manner affect the first and fourth Clauses in the Ninth Section of the first article; and that no State, without its Consent, shall be deprived of its equal Suffrage in the Senate.

Article VI

All Debts contracted and Engagements entered into, before the adoption of this Constitution, shall be as valid against the united States under this Constitution, as under the Confederation.

This Constitution, and the Laws of the united States which shall be made in Pursuance thereof; and all Treaties made, or which shall be made, under the authority of the united States, shall be the supreme Law of the Land; and the Judges in every State shall be bound thereby, any Thing in the Constitution or Laws of any state to the Contrary notwithstanding.

The Senators and Representatives before mentioned, and the Members of the several State Legislatures, and all executive and judicial officers, both of the united States and of the several States, shall be bound by oath or affirmation, to support this Constitution; but no religious Test shall ever be required as a Qualification to any office or public Trust under the united States.

Article VII

The Ratification of the Conventions of nine States, shall be sufficient for the Establishment of this Constitution between the States so ratifying the same.

The Word, "the," being interlined between the seventh and eighth Lines of the first Page, The Word "Thirty" being partly written on an Erazure in the fifteenth Line of the first Page, The Words "is tried" being interlined between the thirty second and thirty third Lines of the first Page and the Word "the" being interlined between the forty third and forty fourth Lines of the second Page.

Attest William Jackson Secretary

done in Convention by the unanimous Consent of the States present the Seventeenth Day of September in the year of our Lord one thousand seven hundred and Eighty seven and of the independance of the united States of america the Twelfth in Witness whereof We have hereunto subscribed our Names,

G°. WASHINGTON—Presid.
and deputy from Virginia

Amendent I

Congress shall make no law respecting an establishment of religion, or prohibiting the free exercise thereof; or abridging the freedom of speech, or of the press; or the right of the people peaceably to assemble, and to petition the Government for a redress of grievances.

Amendment II

A well regulated Militia, being necessary to the security of a free State, the right of the people to keep and bear Arms, shall not be infringed.

Amendment III

No Soldier shall, in time of peace be quartered in any house, without the consent of the Owner, nor in time of war, but in a manner to be prescribed by law.

Amendment IV

The right of the people to be secure in their persons, houses, papers, and effects, against unreasonable searches and seizures, shall not be violated, and no Warrants shall issue, but upon probable cause, supported by Oath or affirmation, and particularly describing the place to be searched, and the persons or things to be seized.

Amendment V

No person shall be held to answer for a capital, or otherwise infamous crime, unless on a presentment or indictment of a Grand Jury, except in cases arising in the land or naval forces, or in the Militia, when in actual service in time of War or public danger; nor shall any person be subject for the same offence to be twice put in jeopardy of life or limb; nor shall be compelled in any criminal case to be a witness against himself, nor be deprived of life, liberty, or property, without due process of law; nor shall private property be taken for public use, without just compensation.

Amendment VI

In all criminal prosecutions, the accused shall enjoy the right to a speedy and public trial, by an impartial jury of the State and district wherein the crime shall have been committed, which district shall have been previously ascertained by law, and to be informed of the nature and cause of the accusation; to be confronted with the witnesses against him; to have compulsory process for obtaining witnesses in his favor, and to have the Assistance of Counsel for his defence.

Amendment VII

In Suits at common law, where the value in controversy shall exceed twenty dollars, the right of trial by jury shall be preserved, and no fact tried by a jury, shall be otherwise re-examined in any Court of the United States, than according to the rules of the common law.

Amendment VIII

Excessive bail shall not be required, nor excessive fines imposed, nor cruel and unusual punishments inflicted.
Amendment IX

The enumeration in the Constitution, of certain rights, shall not be construed to deny or disparage others retained by the people.

Amendment X

The powers not delegated to the United States by the Constitution, nor prohibited by it to the States, are reserved to the States respectively, or to the people.

Amendment XI

(Ratified February 7, 1795)

The Judicial power of the United States shall not be construed to extend to any suit in law or equity, commenced or prosecuted against one of the United States by Citizens of another State, or by Citizens or Subjects of any Foreign State.

Amendment XII

(Ratified June 15, 1804)

The Electors shall meet in their respective states, and vote by ballot for President and Vice-President, one of whom, at least, shall not be an inhabitant of the same state with themselves; they shall name in their ballots the person voted for as President, and in distinct ballots the person voted for as Vice-President, and they shall make distinct lists of all persons voted for as President, and of all persons voted for as Vice-President and of the number of votes for each, which lists they shall sign and certify, and transmit sealed to the seat of the government of the United States, directed to the President of the Senate;

The President of the Senate shall, in the presence of the Senate and House of Representatives, open all the certificates and the votes shall then be counted.

The person having the greatest Number of votes for President, shall be the President, if such number be a majority of the whole number of Electors appointed; and if no person have such majority, then from the persons having the highest numbers not exceeding three on the list of those voted for as President, the House of Representatives shall choose immediately, by ballot, the President. But in choosing the President, the votes shall be taken by states, the representation from each state having one vote; a quorum for this purpose shall consist of a member or members from two-thirds of the states, and a majority of all the states shall be necessary to a choice. And if the House of Representatives shall not choose a President whenever the right of choice shall devolve upon them, before the fourth day of March next following, then the Vice-President shall act as President, as in the case of the death or other constitutional disability of the President.

The person having the greatest number of votes as Vice-President, shall be the Vice-President, if such number be a majority of the whole number of Electors appointed, and if no person have a majority, then from the two highest numbers on the list, the Senate shall choose the Vice-President; a quorum for the purpose shall consist of two-thirds of the whole number of Senators, and a majority of the whole number shall be necessary to a choice. But no person constitutionally ineligible to the office of President shall be eligible to that of Vice-President of the United States.

Amendment XIII

(Ratified December 6, 1865)

Section 1

Neither slavery nor involuntary servitude, except as a punishment for crime whereof the party shall have been duly convicted, shall exist within the United States, or any place subject to their jurisdiction.

Section 2

Congress shall have power to enforce this article by appropriate legislation.

Amendment XIV

(Ratified July 9, 1868)

Section 1

All persons born or naturalized in the United States, and subject to the jurisdiction thereof, are citizens of the United States and of the State wherein they reside. No State shall make or enforce any law which shall abridge the privileges or immunities of citizens of the United States; nor shall any State deprive any person of life, liberty, or property, without due process of law; nor deny to any person within its jurisdiction the equal protection of the laws.

Section 2

Representatives shall be apportioned among the several States according to their respective numbers counting the whole number of persons in each State, excluding Indians not taxed. But when the right to vote at any election for the choice of electors for President and Vice-President of the United States, Representatives in Congress, the Executive and Judicial officers of a State, or the members of the Legislature thereof, is denied to any of the male inhabitants of such State, being twenty-one years of age, and citizens of the United States, or in any way abridged, except for participation in rebellion, or other crime, the basis of representation therein shall be reduced in the proportion which the number of such male citizens shall bear to the whole number of male citizens twenty-one years of age in such State.

Section 3

No person shall be a Senator or Representative in Congress, or elector of President and Vice-President, or hold any office, civil or military, under the United States, or under any State, who, having previously taken an oath, as a member of Congress, or as an officer of the United States, or as a member of any State legislature, or as an executive or judicial officer of any State, to support the Constitution of the United States, shall have engaged in insurrection or rebellion against the same, or given aid or comfort to the enemies thereof. But Congress may by a vote of two-thirds of each House, remove such disability.

Section 4

The validity of the public debt of the United States, authorized by law, including debts incurred for payment of pensions and bounties for services in suppressing insurrection or rebellion, shall not be questioned. But neither the United States nor any State shall assume or pay any debt or obligation incurred in aid of insurrection or rebellion against the United States, or any claim for the loss or emancipation of any slave. But all such debts, obligations and claims shall be held illegal and void.

Section 5

The Congress shall have power to enforce, by appropriate legislation, the provisions of this article.

Amendment XV

(Ratified February 3, 1870)

Section 1

The right of citizens of the United States to vote shall not be denied or abridged by the United States or by any State on account of race, color, or previous condition of servitude.

Section 2

The Congress shall have power to enforce this article by appropriate legislation.

Amendment XVI

(Ratified February 3, 1913)

The Congress shall have power to lay and collect taxes on incomes, from whatever source derived, without apportionment among the several States, and without regard to any census or enumeration.

Amendment XVII

(Ratified April 8, 1913)

The Senate of the United States shall be composed of two Senators from each State, elected by the people thereof, for six years; and each Senator shall have one vote. The electors in each State shall have the qualifications requisite for electors of the most numerous branch of the State legislatures.

When vacancies happen in the representation of any State in the Senate, the executive authority of such State shall issue writs of election to fill such vacancies: Provided, That the legislature of any State may empower the executive thereof to make temporary appointments until the people fill the vacancies by election as the legislature may direct.

This amendment shall not be so construed as to affect the election or term of any Senator chosen before it becomes valid as part of the Constitution.

Amendment XVIII

(Ratified January 16, 1919. Repealed December 5, 1933 with the Ratification of Amendment XXI)

Section 1

After one year from the ratification of this article the manufacture, sale, or transportation of intoxicating liquors within, the importation thereof into, or the exportation thereof from the United States and all territory subject to the jurisdiction thereof for beverage purposes is hereby prohibited.

Section 2

The Congress and all of the several States shall have concurrent power to enforce this article by appropriate legislation.

Section 3

This article shall be inoperative unless it shall have been ratified as an amendment to the Constitution by the legislatures of the several States, as provided in the Constitution, within seven years from the date of the submission hereof to the States by the Congress.

Amendment XIX

(Ratified August 18, 1920)

The right of citizens of the United States to vote shall not be denied or abridged by the United States or by any State on account of sex.

Congress shall have power to enforce this article by appropriate legislation.

Amendment XX

(Ratified January 23, 1933)

Section 1

The terms of the President and Vice President shall end at noon on the 20th day of January, and the terms of Senators and Representatives at noon on the 3d day of January, of the years in which such terms would have ended if this article had not been ratified; and the terms of their successors shall then begin.

Section 2

The Congress shall assemble at least once in every year, and such meeting shall begin at noon on the 3d day of January, unless they shall by law appoint a different day.

Section 3

If, at the time fixed for the beginning of the term of the President, the President elect shall have died, the Vice President elect shall become President. If a President shall not have been chosen before the time fixed for the beginning of his term, or if the President elect shall have failed to qualify, then the Vice President elect shall act as President until a President shall have qualified; and the Congress may by law provide for the case wherein neither a President elect nor a Vice President elect shall have qualified, declaring who shall then act as President, or the manner in which one who is to act shall be selected, and such person shall act accordingly until a President or Vice President shall have qualified.

Section 4

The Congress may by law provide for the case of the death of any of the persons from whom the House of Representatives may choose a President whenever the right of choice shall have devolved upon them, and for the case of the death of any of the persons from whom the Senate may choose a Vice President whenever the right of choice shall have devolved upon them.

Section 5

Sections 1 and 2 shall take effect on the 15th day of October following the ratification of this article.

Section 6

This article shall be inoperative unless it shall have been ratified as an amendment to the Constitution by the legislatures of three-fourths of the several States within seven years from the date of its submission.

Amendment XXI

(Ratified December 5, 1933)

Section 1

The eighteenth article of amendment to the Constitution of the United States is hereby repealed.

Section 2

The transportation or importation into any State, Territory, or possession of the United States for delivery or use therein of intoxicating liquors, in violation of the laws thereof, is hereby prohibited.

Section 3

The article shall be inoperative unless it shall have been ratified as an amendment to the Constitution by conventions in the several States, as provided in the Constitution, within seven years from the date of the submission hereof to the States by the Congress.

Amendment XXII

(Ratified February 27, 1951)

Section 1

No person shall be elected to the office of the President more than twice, and no person who has held the office of President, or acted as President, for more than two years of a term to which some other person was elected President shall be elected to the office of the President more than once. But this Article shall not apply to any person holding the office of President, when this Article was proposed by the Congress, and shall not prevent any person who may be holding the office of President, or acting as President, during the term within which this Article becomes operative from holding the office of President or acting as President during the remainder of such term.

Section 2

This article shall be inoperative unless it shall have been ratified as an amendment to the Constitution by the legislatures of three-fourths of the several States within seven years from the date of its submission to the States by the Congress.

Amendment XXIII

(Ratified March 29, 1961)

Section 1

The District constituting the seat of Government of the United States shall appoint in such manner as the Congress may direct: A number of electors of President and Vice President equal to the whole number of Senators and Representatives in Congress to which the District would be entitled if it were a State, but in no event more than the least populous State; they shall be in addition to those appointed by the States, but they shall be considered, for the purposes of the election of President and Vice President, to be electors appointed by a State; and they shall meet in the District and perform such duties as provided by the twelfth article of amendment.

Section 2

The Congress shall have power to enforce this article by appropriate legislation.

Amendment XXIV

(Ratified January 23, 1964)

Section 1

The right of citizens of the United States to vote in any primary or other election for President or Vice President, for electors for President or Vice President, or for Senator or Representative in Congress, shall not be denied or abridged by the United States or any State by reason of failure to pay any poll tax or other tax.

Section 2
The Congress shall have power to enforce this article by appropriate legislation.

Amendment XXV

(Ratified February 10, 1967)

Section 1
In case of the removal of the President from office or of his death or resignation, the Vice President shall become President.

Section 2
Whenever there is a vacancy in the office of the Vice President, the President shall nominate a Vice President who shall take office upon confirmation by a majority vote of both Houses of Congress.

Section 3
Whenever the President transmits to the President pro tempore of the Senate and the Speaker of the House of Representatives his written declaration that he is unable to discharge the powers and duties of his office, and until he transmits to them a written declaration to the contrary, such powers and duties shall be discharged by the Vice President as Acting President.

Section 4
Whenever the Vice President and a majority of either the principal officers of the executive departments or of such other body as Congress may by law provide, transmit to the President pro tempore of the Senate and the Speaker of the House of Representatives their written declaration that the President is unable to discharge the powers and duties of his office, the Vice President shall immediately assume the powers and duties of the office as Acting President.

Thereafter, when the President transmits to the President pro tempore of the Senate and the Speaker of the House of Representatives his written declaration that no inability exists, he shall resume the powers and duties of his office unless the Vice President and a majority of either the principal officers of the executive department or of such other body as Congress may by law provide, transmit within four days to the President pro tempore of the Senate and the Speaker of the House of Representatives their written declaration that the President is unable to discharge the powers and duties of his office. Thereupon Congress shall decide the issue, assembling within forty eight hours for that purpose if not in session. If the Congress, within twenty one days after receipt of the latter written declaration, or, if Congress is not in session, within twenty one days after Congress is required to assemble, determines by two thirds vote of both Houses that the President is unable to discharge the powers and duties of his office, the Vice President shall continue to discharge the same as Acting President; otherwise, the President shall resume the powers and duties of his office.

Amendment XXVI

(Ratified July 1, 1971)

The right of citizens of the United States, who are eighteen years of age or older, to vote shall not be denied or abridged by the United States or by any State on account of age. Congress shall have the power to enforce this law through appropriate legislation.

Amendment XXVII

(Ratified May 5, 1992)

No law, varying the compensation for the services of the Senators and Representatives, shall take effect, until an election of Representatives shall have intervened.

APPENDIX

D FEDERALIST #10

TO THE PEOPLE OF THE STATE OF NEW YORK:

AMONG the numerous advantages promised by a well-constructed Union, none deserves to be more accurately developed than its tendency to break and control the violence of faction. The friend of popular Governments never finds himself so much alarmed for their character and fate, as when he contemplates their propensity to this dangerous vice. He will not fail, therefore, to set a due value on any plan which, without violating the principles to which he is attached, provides a proper cure for it. The instability, injustice, and confusion introduced into the public councils, have, in truth, been the mortal diseases under which popular Governments have everywhere perished; as they continue to be the favorite and fruitful topics from which the adversaries to liberty derive their most specious declamations. The valuable improvements made by the American Constitutions on the popular models, both ancient and modern, cannot certainly be too much admired; but it would be an unwarrantable partiality, to contend that they have as effectually obviated the danger on this side, as was wished and expected. Complaints are everywhere heard from our most considerate and virtuous citizens, equally the friends of public and private faith, and of public and personal liberty, that our Governments are too unstable; that the public good is disregarded in the conflicts of rival parties; and that measures are too often decided, not according to the rules of justice, and the rights of the minor party, but by the superior force of an interested and overbearing majority. However anxiously we may wish that these complaints had no foundation, the evidence of known facts will not permit us to deny that they are in some degree true. It will be found, indeed, on a candid review of our situation, that some of the distresses under which we labor have been erroneously charged on the operation of our Governments; but it will be found, at the same time, that other causes will not alone account for many of our heaviest misfortunes; and, particularly, for that prevailing and increasing distrust of public engagements, and alarm for private rights, which are echoed from one end of the continent to the other. These must be chiefly, if not wholly, effects of the unsteadiness and injustice, with which a factious spirit has tainted our public administrations.

By a faction, I understand a number of citizens, whether amounting to a majority or a minority of the whole, who are united and actuated by some common impulse of passion, or of interest, adverse to the rights of other citizens, or to the permanent and aggregate interests of the community.

There are two methods of curing the mischiefs of faction: the one, by removing its causes; the other, by controlling its effects.

There are again two methods of removing the causes of faction: the one, by destroying the liberty which is essential to its existence; the other, by giving to every citizen the same opinions, the same passions, and the same interests.

It could never be more truly said than of the first remedy, that it was worse than the disease. Liberty is to faction what air is to fire, an aliment without which it instantly expires. But it could not be less folly to abolish liberty, which is essential to political life, because it nourishes faction, than it would be to wish the annihilation of air, which is essential to animal life, because it imparts to fire its destructive agency.

The second expedient is as impracticable, as the first would be unwise. As long as the reason of man continues fallible, and he is at liberty to exercise it, different opinions will be formed. As long as the connection subsists between his reason and his self-love, his opinions and his passions will have a reciprocal influence on each other; and the former will be objects to which the latter will attach themselves. The diversity in the faculties of men, from which the rights of property originate, is not less an insuperable obstacle to a uniformity of interests. The protection of these faculties is the first object of Government. From the protection of different and unequal faculties of acquiring property, the possession of different degrees and kinds of property immediately results; and from the influence of these on the sentiments and views of the respective proprietors, ensues a division of the society into different interests and parties.

The latent causes of faction are thus sown in the nature of man; and we see them everywhere brought into different degrees of activity, according to the different circumstances of civil society. A zeal for different opinions concerning religion, concerning Government, and many other points, as well of speculation as of practice; an attachment to different leaders ambitiously contending for preëminence and power; or to persons of other descriptions whose fortunes have been interesting to the human passions, have, in turn, divided mankind into parties, inflamed them with mutual animosity, and rendered them much more disposed to vex and oppress each other, than to coöperate for their common good. So strong is this propensity of mankind to fall into mutual animosities, that where no substantial occasion presents itself, the most frivolous and fanciful distinctions have been sufficient to kindle their unfriendly passions, and excite their most violent conflicts. But the most common and durable source of factions has been the various and unequal distribution of property. Those who hold, and those who are without property, have ever formed distinct interests in society. Those who are creditors, and those who are debtors, fall under a like discrimination. A landed interest, a manufacturing interest, a mercantile interest, a moneyed interest, with many lesser interests, grow up of necessity in civilized nations, and divide them into different classes, actuated by different sentiments and views. The regulation of these various and interfering interests forms the principal task of modern Legislation, and involves the spirit of party and faction in the necessary and ordinary operations of the Government.

No man is allowed to be a judge in his own cause; because his interest would certainly bias his judgment, and, not improbably, corrupt his integrity. With equal, nay with greater reason, a body of men are unfit to be both judges and parties at the same time; yet what are many of the most important acts of legislation, but so many judicial determinations, not indeed concerning the rights of single persons, but concerning the rights of large bodies of citizens? and what are the different classes of Legislators, but advocates and parties to the causes which they determine? Is a law proposed concerning private debts? It is a question to which the creditors are parties on one side and the debtors on the other. Justice ought to hold the balance between them. Yet the parties are, and must be, themselves the judges; and the most numerous party, or, in other words, the most powerful faction, must be expected to prevail. Shall domestic manufactures be encouraged, and in what degree, by restrictions on foreign manufactures? are questions which would be differently decided by the landed and the manufacturing classes; and probably by neither, with a sole regard to justice and the public good. The apportionment of taxes on the various descriptions of property is an act which seems to require the most exact impartiality; yet there is, perhaps, no legislative act in which greater opportunity and temptation are given to a predominant party, to trample on the rules of justice. Every shilling, with which they overburden the inferior number, is a shilling saved to their own pockets.

It is in vain to say, that enlightened statesmen will be able to adjust these clashing interests, and render them all subservient to the public good. Enlightened statesmen will not always be at the helm: Nor, in many cases, can such an adjustment be made at all, without taking into view indirect and remote considerations, which will rarely prevail over the immediate interest which one party may find in disregarding the rights of another, or the good of the whole.

The inference to which we are brought is, that the *causes* of faction cannot be removed; and that relief is only to be sought in the means of controlling its *effects*.

If a faction consists of less than a majority, relief is supplied by the republican principle, which enables the majority to defeat its sinister views by regular vote. It may clog the administration, it may convulse the society; but it will be unable to execute and mask its violence under the forms of the Constitution. When a majority is included in a faction, the form of popular Government, on the other hand, enables it to sacrifice to its ruling passion or interest both the public good and the rights of other citizens. To secure the public good, and private rights, against the danger of such a faction, and at the same time to preserve the spirit and the form of popular Government, is then the great object to which our inquiries are directed: Let me add, that it is the great desideratum, by which this form of Government can be rescued from the opprobrium under which it has so long labored, and be recommended to the esteem and adoption of mankind.

By what means is this object attainable? Evidently by one of two only. Either the existence of the same passion or interest in a majority, at the same time, must be prevented; or the majority, having such coexistent passion or interest, must be rendered, by their number and local situation, unable to concert and carry into effect schemes of oppression. If the impulse and the opportunity be suffered to coincide, we well know that neither moral nor religious motives can be relied on as an adequate control. They are not found to be such on the injustice and violence of individuals, and lose their efficacy in proportion to the number combined together; that is, in proportion as their efficacy becomes needful.

From this view of the subject, it may be concluded, that a pure Democracy, by which I mean a Society consisting of a small number of citizens, who assemble and administer the Government in person, can admit of no cure for the mischiefs of faction. A common passion or interest will, in almost every case, be felt by a majority of the whole; a communication and concert result from the form of Government itself; and there is nothing to check the inducements to sacrifice the weaker party, or an obnoxious individual. Hence it is, that such Democracies have ever been spectacles of turbulence and contention; have ever been found incompatible with personal security, or the rights of property; and have in general been as short in their lives, as they have been violent in their deaths. Theoretic politicians, who have patronized this species of Government, have erroneously supposed, that by reducing mankind to a perfect equality in their political rights, they would, at the same time, be perfectly equalized and assimilated in their possessions, their opinions, and their passions.

A Republic, by which I mean a Government in which the scheme of representation takes place, opens a different prospect, and promises the cure for which we are seeking. Let us examine the points in which it varies from pure Democracy, and we shall comprehend both the nature of the cure, and the efficacy which it must derive from the Union.

The two great points of difference, between a Democracy and a Republic, are, first, the delegation of the Government, in the latter, to a small number of citizens elected by the rest: Secondly, the greater number of citizens, and greater sphere of country, over which the latter may be extended.

The effect of the first difference is, on the one hand, to refine and enlarge the public views, by passing them through the medium of a chosen body of citizens, whose wisdom may best discern the true interest of their country, and whose patriotism and love of justice will be least likely to sacrifice it to temporary or partial considerations. Under such a regulation, it may well happen, that the public voice, pronounced by the representatives of the People, will be more consonant to the public good, than if pronounced by the People themselves, convened for the purpose. On the other hand, the effect may be inverted. Men of factious tempers, of local prejudices, or of sinister designs, may by intrigue, by corruption, or by other means, first obtain the suffrages, and then betray the interests of the people. The question resulting is, whether small or extensive Republics are more favorable to the election of proper guardians of the public weal; and it is clearly decided in favor of the latter by two obvious considerations.

In the first place, it is to be remarked that however small the Republic may be, the Representatives must be raised to a certain number, in order to guard against the cabals of a few; and that however large it may be, they must be limited to a certain number, in order to guard against the confusion of a multitude. Hence, the number of Representatives in the two cases not being in proportion to that of the Constituents, and being proportionally greater in the small Republic, it follows, that if the proportion of fit characters be not less in the large than in the small Republic, the former will present a greater option, and consequently a greater probability of a fit choice.

In the next place, as each Representative will be chosen by a greater number of citizens in the large than in the small Republic, it will be more difficult for unworthy candidates to practise with success the vicious arts, by which elections are too often carried; and the suffrages of the People, being more free, will be more likely to centre in men who possess the most attractive merit, and the most diffusive and established characters.

It must be confessed, that in this, as in most other cases, there is a mean, on both sides of which inconveniences will be found to lie. By enlarging too much the number of electors, you render the representatives too little acquainted with all their local circumstances and lesser interests; as by reducing it too much, you render him unduly attached to these, and too little fit to comprehend and pursue great and National objects. The Fœderal Constitution forms a happy combination in this respect; the great and aggregate interests being referred to the National, the local and particular to the State Legislatures.

The other point of difference is, the greater number of citizens and extent of territory which may be brought within the compass of Republican, than of Democratic Government; and it is this circumstance principally which renders factious combinations less to be dreaded in the former, than in the latter. The smaller the society, the fewer probably will be the distinct parties and interests composing it; the fewer the distinct parties and interests, the more frequently will a majority be found of the same party; and the smaller the number of individuals composing a majority, and the smaller the compass within which they are placed, the more easily will they concert and execute their plans of oppression. Extend the sphere, and you take in a greater variety of parties and interests; you make it less probable that a majority of the whole will have a common motive to invade the rights of other citizens; or if such a common motive exists, it will be more difficult for all who feel it to discover their own strength, and to act in unison with each other. Besides other impediments, it may be remarked, that where there is a consciousness of unjust or dishonorable purposes, communication is always checked by distrust, in proportion to the number whose concurrence is necessary.

Hence, it clearly appears, that the same advantage which a Republic has over a Democracy, in controlling the effects of faction, is enjoyed by a large over a small Republic,—is enjoyed by the Union over the States composing it. Does the advantage consist in the substitution of Representatives, whose enlightened views and virtuous sentiments render them superior to local prejudices, and to schemes of injustice? It will not be denied, that the Representation of the Union will be most likely to possess these requisite endowments. Does it consist in the greater security afforded by a greater variety of parties, against the event of any one party being able to outnumber and oppress the rest? In an equal degree does the increased variety of parties, comprised within the Union, increase this security. Does it, in fine, consist in the greater obstacles opposed to the concert and accomplishment of the secret wishes of an unjust and interested majority? Here, again, the extent of the Union gives it the most palpable advantage.

The influence of factious leaders may kindle a flame within their particular States, but will be unable to spread a general conflagration through the other States: A religious sect may degenerate into a political faction in a part of the Confederacy; but the variety of sects dispersed over the entire face of it, must secure the National Councils against any danger from that source; A rage for paper money, for an abolition of debts, for an equal division of property, or for any other improper or wicked project, will be less apt to pervade the whole body of the Union, than a particular member of it; in the same proportion as such a malady is more likely to taint a particular county or district, than an entire State.

In the extent and proper structure of the Union, therefore, we behold a Republican remedy for the diseases most incident to Republican Government. And according to the degree of pleasure and pride we feel in being Republicans, ought to be our zeal in cherishing the spirit, and supporting the character, of Fœderalists.

PUBLIUS.

E FEDERALIST #47

TO THE PEOPLE OF THE STATE OF NEW YORK:

IT was shown in the last paper, that the political apophthegm there examined does not require that the Legislative, Executive, and Judiciary departments should be wholly unconnected with each other. I shall undertake in the next place to show, that unless these departments be so far connected and blended, as to give to each a constitutional control over the others, the degree of separation which the maxim requires, as essential to a free Government, can never in practice be duly maintained.

It is agreed on all sides, that the powers properly belonging to one of the departments ought not to be directly and completely administered by either of the other departments. It is equally evident, that none of them ought to possess, directly or indirectly, an overruling influence over the others in the administration of their respective powers. It will not be denied, that power is of an encroaching nature, and that it ought to be effectually restrained from passing the limits assigned to it. After discriminating, therefore, in theory, the several classes of power as they may in their nature be Legislative, Executive, or Judiciary, the next and most difficult task is to provide some practical security for each, against the invasion of the others. What this security ought to be, is the great problem to be solved.

Will it be sufficient to mark, with precision, the boundaries of these departments, in the constitution of the Government, and to trust to these parchment barriers against the encroaching spirit of power? This is the security which appears to have been principally relied on by the compilers of most of the American Constitutions. But experience assures us, that the efficacy of the provision has been greatly overrated; and that some more adequate defence is indispensably necessary for the more feeble, against the more powerful, members of the Government. The Legislative department is everywhere extending the sphere of its activity, and drawing all power into its impetuous vortex.

The founders of our republics have so much merit for the wisdom which they have displayed, that no task can be less pleasing than that of pointing out the errors into which they have fallen. A respect for truth, however, obliges us to remark, that they seem never for a moment to have turned their eyes from the danger to liberty from the overgrown and all-grasping prerogative of an hereditary magistrate, supported and fortified by an hereditary branch of the Legislative authority. They seem never to have recollected the danger from Legislative usurpations, which, by assembling all power in the same hands, must lead to the same tyranny as is threatened by Executive usurpations.

In a Government where numerous and extensive prerogatives are placed in the hands of an hereditary monarch, the Executive department is very justly regarded as the source of danger, and watched with all the jealousy which a zeal for liberty ought to inspire. In a democracy, where a multitude of people exercise in person the Legislative functions, and are continually exposed, by their incapacity for regular deliberation and concerted measures, to the ambitious intrigues of their Executive magistrates, tyranny may well be apprehended, on some favorable emergency, to start up in the same quarter. But in a representative republic, where the Executive magistracy is carefully limited, both in the extent and the duration of its power; and where the Legislative power is exercised by an assembly, which is inspired, by a supposed influence over the People, with an intrepid confidence in its own strength; which is sufficiently numerous to feel all the passions which actuate a multitude, yet not so numerous as to be incapable of pursuing the objects of its passions, by means which reason prescribes; it is against the enterprising ambition of this department, that the People ought to indulge all their jealousy, and exhaust all their precautions.

The Legislative department derives a superiority in our Governments from other circumstances. Its constitutional powers being at once more extensive, and less susceptible of precise limits, it can, with the greater facility, mask, under complicated and indirect measures, the encroachments which it makes on the coördinate departments. It is not unfrequently a question of real nicety in Legislative bodies, whether the operation of a particular measure will, or will not extend beyond the Legislative sphere. On the other side, the Executive power being restrained within a narrower compass, and being more simple in its nature, and the Judiciary being described by landmarks, still less uncertain, projects of usurpation by either of these departments would immediately betray and defeat themselves. Nor is this all: as the Legislative department alone has access to the pockets of the People, and has in some Constitutions full discretion, and in all a prevailing influence over the pecuniary rewards of those who fill the other departments, a dependence is thus created in the latter, which gives still greater facility to encroachments of the former.

I have appealed to our own experience for the truth of what I advance on this subject. Were it necessary to verify this experience by particular proofs, they might be multiplied without end. I might find a witness in every citizen who has shared in, or been attentive to, the course of public administrations. I might collect vouchers in abundance from the records and archives of every State in the Union. But as a more concise, and at the same time equally satisfactory evidence, I will refer to the example of two States, attested by two unexceptionable authorities.

The first example is that of Virginia, a State which, as we have seen, has expressly declared in its Constitution, that the three great departments ought not to be intermixed. The authority in support of it is Mr. Jefferson, who, besides his other advantages for remarking the operation of the Government, was himself the chief magistrate of it. In order to convey fully the ideas with which his experience had impressed him on this subject, it will be necessary to quote a passage of some length from his very interesting "Notes on the State of Virginia," p. 195. "All the powers of Government, Legislative, Executive, and Judiciary, result to the Legislative body. The concentrating these in the same hands, is precisely the definition, of despotic Government. It will be no alleviation, that these powers will be exercised by a plurality of hands, and not by a single one. One hundred and seventy-three despots would surely be as oppressive as one. Let those who doubt it, turn their eyes on the republic of Venice. As little will it avail us, that they are chosen by ourselves. An *elective despotism* was not the Government we fought for; but one which should not only be founded on free principles, but in which the powers of Government should be so divided and balanced among several bodies of magistracy, as that no one could transcend their legal limits, without being effectually checked and restrained by the others. For this reason, that Convention which passed the ordinance of Government, laid its foundation on this basis, that the Legislative, Executive, and Judiciary departments should be separate and distinct, so that no person should exercise the powers of more than one of them at the same time. *But no barrier was provided between these several powers.* The Judiciary and Executive members were left dependent on the Legislative for their subsistence in office, and some of them for their continuance in it. If, therefore, the Legislature assumes Executive and Judiciary powers, no opposition is likely to be made; nor, if made, can be effectual; because in that case they may put their proceeding into the form of an Act of Assembly, which will render them obligatory on the other branches. They have accordingly, *in many* instances, *decided rights*, which should have been left to *Judiciary controversy;* and *the direction of the Executive, during the whole time of their session, is becoming habitual and familiar.*"

The other State which I shall take for an example is Pennsylvania; and the other authority, the Council of Censors which assembled in the years 1783 and 1784. A part of the duty of this body, as marked out by the Constitution, was "to inquire whether the Constitution had been preserved inviolate in every part; and whether the Legislative and Executive branches of Government had performed their duty as guardians of the People, or assumed to themselves, or exercised other or greater powers than they are entitled to by the Constitution." In the execution of this trust, the Council were necessarily led to a comparison of both the Legislative and Executive proceedings, with the constitutional powers of these departments; and from the facts enumerated, and to the truth of most of which both sides in the Council subscribed, it appears, that the Constitution had been flagrantly violated by the Legislature in a variety of important instances.

A great number of laws had been passed, violating, without any apparent necessity, the rule requiring that all bills of a public nature shall be previously printed for the consideration of the People; although this is one of the precautions chiefly relied on by the Constitution against improper acts of Legislature.

The constitutional trial by jury had been violated; and powers assumed, which had not been delegated by the Constitution.

Executive powers had been usurped.

The salaries of the Judges, which the Constitution expressly requires to be fixed, had been occasionally varied; and cases belonging to the Judiciary department frequently drawn within Legislative cognizance and determination.

Those who wish to see the several particulars falling under each of these heads, may consult the Journals of the Council, which are in print. Some of them, it will be found, may be imputable to peculiar circumstances connected with the war; but the greater part of them may be considered as the spontaneous shoots of an ill-constituted Government.

It appears, also, that the Executive department had not been innocent of frequent breaches of the Constitution. There are three observations, however, which ought to be made on this head: *First*, A great proportion of the instances were either immediately produced by the necessities of the war, or recommended by Congress, or the Commander-in-chief; *Secondly*, In most of the other instances, they conformed either to the declared or the known sentiments of the Legislative department; *Thirdly*, The Executive department of Pennsylvania is distinguished from that of the other States, by the number of members composing it. In this respect, it has as much affinity to a Legislative assembly, as to an Executive Council. And being at once exempt from the restraint of an individual responsibility for the acts of the body, and deriving confidence from mutual example and joint influence, unauthorized measures would of course be more freely hazarded, than where the Executive department is administered by a single hand, or by a few hands.

The conclusion which I am warranted in drawing from these observations is, that a mere demarcation on parchment of the constitutional limits of the several departments is not a sufficient guard against those encroachments which lead to a tyrannical concentration of all the powers of Government in the same hands.

PUBLIUS.

F FEDERALIST #48

TO THE PEOPLE OF THE STATE OF NEW YORK:

THE author of the "Notes on the State of Virginia," quoted in the last paper, has subjoined to that valuable work the draught of a Constitution, which had been prepared in order to be laid before a Convention expected to be called in 1783, by the Legislature, for the establishment of a Constitution for that Commonwealth. The plan, like everything from the same pen, marks a turn of thinking, original, comprehensive, and accurate; and is the more worthy of attention as it equally displays a fervent attachment to republican Government, and an enlightened view of the dangerous propensities against which it ought to be guarded. One of the precautions which he proposes, and on which he appears ultimately to rely as a palladium to the weaker departments of power, against the invasions of the stronger is perhaps altogether his own, and as it immediately relates to the subject of our present inquiry, ought not to be overlooked.

His proposition is, "that whenever any two of the three branches of Government shall concur in opinion, each by the voices of two thirds of their whole number, that a Convention is necessary for altering the Constitution, or *correcting breaches of it*, a Convention shall be called for the purpose."

As the People are the only legitimate fountain of power, and it is from them that the constitutional charter, under which the several branches of Government hold their power, is derived, it seems strictly consonant to the republican theory, to recur to the same original authority, not only whenever it may be necessary to enlarge, diminish, or new-model the powers of the Government; but also whenever any one of the departments may commit encroachments on the chartered authorities of the others. The several departments being perfectly coördinate by the terms of their common commission, neither of them, it is evident, can pretend to an exclusive or superior right of settling the boundaries between their respective powers; and how are the encroachments of the stronger to be prevented, or the wrongs of the weaker to be redressed, without an appeal to the People themselves, who, as the grantors of the commission, can alone declare its true meaning, and enforce its observance?

There is certainly great force in this reasoning, and it must be allowed to prove that a constitutional road to the decision of the People ought to be marked out and kept open, for certain great and extraordinary occasions. But there appear to be insuperable objections against the proposed recurrence to the People, as a provision in all cases for keeping the several departments of power within their constitutional limits.

In the first place, the provision does not reach the case of a combination of two of the departments against a third. If the Legislative authority, which possesses so many means of operating on the motives of the other departments, should be able to gain to its interest either of the others, or even one third of its members, the remaining department could derive no advantage from its remedial provision. I do not dwell, however, on this objection, because it may be thought to lie rather against the modification of the principle, than against the principle itself.

In the next place, it may be considered as an objection inherent in the principle, that as every appeal to the People would carry an implication of some defect in the Government, frequent appeals would, in a great measure, deprive the Government of that veneration which time bestows on everything, and without which perhaps the wisest and freest Governments would not possess the requisite stability. If it be true that all Governments rest on opinion, it is no less true, that the strength of opinion in each individual, and its practical influence on his conduct, depend much on the number which he supposes to have entertained the same opinion. The reason of man, like man himself, is timid and cautious when left alone; and acquires firmness and confidence, in proportion to the number with which it is associated. When the examples which fortify opinion are *ancient*, as well as *numerous*, they are known to have a double effect. In a Nation of philosophers, this consideration ought to be disregarded. A reverence for the laws would be sufficiently inculcated by the voice of an enlightened reason. But a Nation of philosophers is as little to be expected as the philosophical race of kings wished for by Plato. And in every other Nation, the most rational Government will not find it a superfluous advantage to have the prejudices of the community on its side.

The danger of disturbing the public tranquillity by interesting too strongly the public passions, is a still more serious objection against a frequent reference of constitutional questions to the decision of the whole society. Notwithstanding the success which has attended the revisions of our established forms of Government, and which does so much honor to the virtue and intelligence of the People of America, it must be confessed, that the experiments are of too ticklish a nature to be unnecessarily multiplied. We are to recollect, that all the existing Constitutions were formed in the midst of a danger which repressed the passions most unfriendly to order and concord; of an enthusiastic confidence of the People in their patriotic leaders, which stifled the ordinary diversity of opinions on great National questions; of a universal ardor for new and opposite forms, produced by a universal resentment and indignation against the ancient Government; and whilst no spirit of party, connected with the changes to be made, or the abuses to be reformed, could mingle its leaven in the operation. The future situations in which we must expect to be usually placed, do not present any equivalent security against the danger which is apprehended.

But the greatest objection of all is, that the decisions which would probably result from such appeals would not answer the purpose of maintaining the constitutional equilibrium of the Government. We have seen that the tendency of republican Governments is to an aggrandizement of the Legislative, at the expense of the other departments. The appeals to the People, therefore, would usually be made by the Executive and Judiciary departments. But whether made by one side or the other, would each side enjoy equal advantages on the trial? Let us view their different situations. The members of the Executive and Judiciary departments are few in number, and can be personally known to a small part only of the People. The latter, by the mode of their appointment, as well as by the nature and permanency of it, are too far removed from the People to share much in their prepossessions. The former are generally the objects of jealousy; and their administration is always liable to be discolored and rendered unpopular. The members of the Legislative department, on the other hand, are numerous. They are distributed and dwell among the People at large. Their connections of blood, of friendship, and of acquaintance, embrace a great proportion of the most influential part of the society. The nature of their public trust implies a personal influence among the People, and that they are more immediately the confidential guardians of the rights and liberties of the People. With these advantages, it can hardly be supposed that the adverse party would have an equal chance for a favorable issue.

But the Legislative party would not only be able to plead their cause most successfully with the People. They would probably be constituted themselves the judges. The same influence which had gained them an election into the Legislature, would gain them a seat in the Convention. If this should not be the case with all, it would probably be the case with many, and pretty certainly with those leading characters, on whom every thing depends in such bodies. The Convention, in short, would be composed chiefly of men who had been, who actually were, or who expected to be, members of the department whose conduct was arraigned. They would consequently be parties to the very question to be decided by them.

It might, however, sometimes happen, that appeals would be made under circumstances less adverse to the Executive and Judiciary departments. The usurpations of the Legislature might be so flagrant and so sudden, as to admit of no specious coloring. A strong party among themselves might take side with the other branches. The Executive power might be in the hands of a peculiar favorite of the People. In such a posture of things, the public decision might be less swayed by prepossessions in favor of the Legislative party. But still it could never be expected to turn on the true merits of the question. It would inevitably be connected with the spirit of preëxisting parties, or of parties springing out of the question itself. It would be connected with persons of distinguished character, and extensive influence in the community. It would be pronounced by the very men who had been agents in, or opponents of the measures, to which the decision would relate. The *passions*, therefore, not the *reason*, of the public, would sit in judgment. But it is the reason of the public alone, that ought to control and regulate the Government. The passions ought to be controlled and regulated by the Government.

We found in the last paper, that mere declarations in the written Constitution are not sufficient to restrain the several departments within their legal rights. It appears in this, that occasional appeals to the People would be neither a proper, nor an effectual provision for that purpose. How far the provisions of a different nature contained in the plan above quoted might be adequate, I do not examine. Some of them are unquestionably founded on sound political principles, and all of them are framed with singular ingenuity and precision.

PUBLIUS.

G FEDERALIST #51

TO THE PEOPLE OF THE STATE OF NEW YORK:

FROM the more general inquiries pursued in the four last papers, I pass on to a more particular examination of the several parts of the Government. I shall begin with the House of Representatives.

The first view to be taken of this part of the Government relates to the qualifications of the electors and the elected.

Those of the former are to be the same with those of the electors of the most numerous branch of the State Legislatures. The definition of the right of suffrage is very justly regarded as a fundamental article of republican Government. It was incumbent on the Convention, therefore, to define and establish this right in the Constitution. To have left it open for the occasional regulation of the Congress, would have been improper for the reason just mentioned. To have submitted it to the Legislative discretion of the States, would have been improper for the same reason; and for the additional reason that it would have rendered too dependent on the State Governments, that branch of the Fœderal Government which ought to be dependent on the People alone. To have reduced the different qualifications in the different States to one uniform rule, would probably have been as dissatisfactory to some of the States, as it would have been difficult to the Convention. The provision made by the Convention appears, therefore, to be the best that lay within their option. It must be satisfactory to every State; because it is conformable to the standard already established, or which may be established by the State itself. It will be safe to the United States; because, being fixed by the State Constitutions, it is not alterable by the State Governments, and it cannot be feared that the People of the States will alter this part of their Constitutions in such a manner as to abridge the rights secured to them by the Fœderal Constitution.

The qualifications of the elected, being less carefully and properly defined by the State Constitutions, and being at the same time more susceptible of uniformity, have been very properly considered and regulated by the Convention. A representative of the United States must be of the age of twenty-five years; must have been seven years a citizen of the United States; must, at the time of his election, be an inhabitant of the State he is to represent; and, during the time of his service, must be in no office under the United States. Under these reasonable limitations, the door of this part of the Fœderal Government is open to merit of every description, whether native or adoptive, whether young or old, and without regard to poverty or wealth, or to any particular profession of religious faith.

The term for which the Representatives are to be elected, falls under a second view which may be taken of this branch. In order to decide on the propriety of this Article, two questions must be considered: First, whether biennial elections will, in this case, be safe; Secondly, whether they be necessary or useful.

First. As it is essential to liberty, that the Government in general should have a common interest with the People; so it is particularly essential, that the branch of it under consideration should have an immediate dependence on, and an intimate sympathy with the People. Frequent elections are unquestionably the only policy by which this dependence and sympathy can be effectually secured. But what particular degree of frequency may be absolutely necessary for the purpose, does not appear to be susceptible of any precise calculation, and must depend on a variety of circumstances with which it may be connected. Let us consult experience, the guide that ought always to be followed, whenever it can be found.

The scheme of representation, as a substitute for a meeting of the citizens in person, being at most but very imperfectly known to ancient polity, it is in more modern times only, that we are to expect instructive examples. And even here, in order to avoid a research too vague and diffusive, it will be proper to confine ourselves to the few examples which are best known, and which bear the greatest analogy to our particular case. The first to which this character ought to be applied, is the House of Commons in Great Britain. The history of this branch of the English Constitution, anterior to the date of Magna Charta, is too obscure to yield instruction. The very existence of it has been made a question among political antiquaries. The earliest records of subsequent date prove, that Parliaments were to *sit* only every year; not that they were to be *elected* every year. And even these annual sessions were left so much at the discretion of the monarch, that under various pretexts, very long and dangerous intermissions were often contrived by royal ambition. To remedy this grievance, it was provided by a statute in the reign of Charles II., that the intermissions should not be protracted beyond a period of three years. On the accession of William III., when a revolution took place in the Government, the subject was still more seriously resumed, and it was declared to be among the fundamental rights of the People, that Parliaments ought to be held *frequently*. By another statute, which passed a few years later in the same reign, the term "frequently," which had alluded to the triennial period settled in the time of Charles II., is reduced to a precise meaning, it being expressly enacted, that a new Parliament shall be called within three years after the determination of the former. The last change, from three to seven years, is well known to have been introduced pretty early in the present century, under an alarm for the Hanoverian succession. From these facts it appears, that the greatest frequency of elections which has been deemed necessary in that kingdom, for binding the Representatives to their constituents, does not exceed a triennial return of them. And if we may argue from the degree of liberty retained even under septennial elections, and all the other vicious ingredients in the Parliamentary

Constitution, we cannot doubt that a reduction of the period from seven to three years, with the other necessary reforms, would so far extend the influence of the People over their Representatives as to satisfy us, that biennial elections, under the Fœderal system, cannot possibly be dangerous to the requisite dependence of the House of Representatives on their constituents.

Elections in Ireland, till of late, were regulated entirely by the discretion of the crown, and were seldom repeated, except on the accession of a new Prince, or some other contingent event. The Parliament which commenced with George II. was continued throughout his whole reign, a period of about thirty-five years. The only dependence of the Representatives on the People consisted in the right of the latter to supply occasional vacancies, by the election of new members, and in the chance of some event which might produce a general new election. The ability also of the Irish Parliament to maintain the rights of their constituents, so far as the disposition might exist, was extremely shackled by the control of the crown over the subjects of their deliberation. Of late these shackles, if I mistake not, have been broken; and octennial Parliaments have besides been established. What effect may be produced by this partial reform, must be left to further experience. The example of Ireland, from this view of it, can throw but little light on the subject. As far as we can draw any conclusion from it, it must be that if the People of that country have been able under all these disadvantages to retain any liberty whatever, the advantage of biennial elections would secure to them every degree of liberty, which might depend on a due connection between their Representatives and themselves.

Let us bring our inquiries nearer home. The example of these States, when British colonies, claims particular attention, at the same time that it is so well known as to require little to be said on it. The principle of representation, in one branch of the Legislature at least, was established in all of them. But the periods of election were different. They varied from one to seven years. Have we any reason to infer from the spirit and conduct of the Representatives of the People, prior to the Revolution, that biennial elections would have been dangerous to the public liberties? The spirit which everywhere displayed itself, at the commencement of the struggle, and which vanquished the obstacles to Independence, is the best of proofs, that a sufficient portion of liberty had been everywhere enjoyed, to inspire both a sense of its worth and a zeal for its proper enlargement. This remark holds good, as well with regard to the then colonies whose elections were least frequent, as to those whose elections were most frequent. Virginia was the colony which stood first in resisting the Parliamentary usurpations of Great Britain; it was the first also in espousing, by public Act, the resolution of Independence. In Virginia, nevertheless, if I have not been misinformed, elections under the former Government were septennial. This particular example is brought into view, not as a proof of any peculiar merit, for the priority in those instances was probably accidental; and still less of any advantage in *septennial* elections, for when compared with a greater frequency they are inadmissible; but merely as a proof, and I conceive it to be a very substantial proof, that the liberties of the People can be in no danger from *biennial* elections.

The conclusion resulting from these examples will be not a little strengthened, by recollecting three circumstances. The first is, that the Fœderal Legislature will possess a part only of that supreme Legislative authority which is vested completely in the British Parliament; and which, with a few exceptions, was exercised by the colonial Assemblies and the Irish Legislature. It is a received and well-founded maxim, that where no other circumstances affect the case, the greater the power is, the shorter ought to be its duration; and conversely, the smaller the power, the more safely may its duration be protracted. In the second place, it has, on another occasion, been shown, that the Fœderal Legislature will not only be restrained by its dependence on the People as other Legislative bodies are, but that it will be moreover watched and controlled by the several collateral Legislatures, which other Legislative bodies are not. And in the third place, no comparison can be made between the means that will be possessed by the more permanent branches of the Fœderal Government, for seducing, if they should be disposed to seduce, the House of Representatives from their duty to the People, and the means of influence over the popular branch, possessed by the other branches of the Government above cited. With less power, therefore, to abuse, the Fœderal Representatives can be less tempted on one side, and will be doubly watched on the other.

PUBLIUS.

H FEDERALIST #78

TO THE PEOPLE OF THE STATE OF NEW YORK:

WE proceed now to an examination of the Judiciary department of the proposed Government.

In unfolding the defects of the existing Confederation the utility and necessity of a Fœderal Judicature have been clearly pointed out. It is the less necessary to recapitulate the considerations there urged, as the propriety of the institution in the abstract is not disputed; the only questions which have been raised being relative to the manner of constituting it, and to its extent. To these points, therefore, our observations shall be confined.

The manner of constituting it seems to embrace these several objects:—1st. The mode of appointing the Judges;—2d. The tenure by which they are to hold their places;—3d. The partition of the Judiciary authority between different courts, and their relations to each other.

First. As to the mode of appointing the Judges; this is the same with that of appointing the officers of the Union in general, and has been so fully discussed in the two last numbers, that nothing can be said here which would not be useless repetition.

Second. As to the tenure by which the Judges are to hold their places: this chiefly concerns their duration in office; the provisions for their support; the precautions for their responsibility.

According to the plan of the Convention, all Judges who may be appointed by the United States are to hold their offices *during good behavior;* which is conformable to the most approved of the State Constitutions, and among the rest, to that of this State. Its propriety having been drawn into question by the adversaries of that plan, is no light symptom of the rage for objection, which disorders their imaginations and judgments. The standard of good behavior for the continuance in office of the Judicial magistracy, is certainly one of the most valuable of the modern improvements in the practice of Government. In a monarchy, it is an excellent barrier to the despotism of the Prince; in a republic it is a no less excellent barrier to the encroachments and oppressions of the representative body. And it is the best expedient which can be devised in any Government, to secure a steady, upright, and impartial administration of the laws.

Whoever attentively considers the different departments of power must perceive, that, in a Government in which they are separated from each other, the Judiciary, from the nature of its functions, will always be the least dangerous to the political rights of the Constitution; because it will be least in a capacity to annoy or injure them. The Executive not only dispenses the honors, but holds the sword of the community. The Legislature not only commands the purse, but prescribes the rules by which the duties and rights of every citizen are to be regulated. The Judiciary, on the contrary, has no influence over either the sword or the purse; no direction either of the strength or of the wealth of the society; and can take no active resolution whatever. It may truly be said to have neither force nor will, but merely judgment; and must ultimately depend upon the aid of the Executive arm even for the efficacy of its judgments.

This simple view of the matter suggests several important consequences. It proves incontestably, that the Judiciary is beyond comparison the weakest of the three departments of power;1 that it can never attack with success either of the other two; and that all possible care is requisite to enable it to defend itself against their attacks. It equally proves, that though individual oppression may now and then proceed from the courts of justice, the general liberty of the People can never be endangered from that quarter: I mean so long as the Judiciary remains truly distinct from both the Legislature and the Executive. For I agree, that "there is no liberty, if the power of judging be not separated from the Legislative and Executive powers."2 And it proves, in the last place, that as liberty can have nothing to fear from the Judiciary alone, but would have everything to fear from its union with either of the other departments; that as all the effects of such an union must ensue from a dependence of the former on the latter, notwithstanding a nominal and apparent separation; that as, from the natural feebleness of the Judiciary, it is in continual jeopardy of being overpowered, awed, or influenced by its coördinate branches; and that as nothing can contribute so much to its firmness and independence as permanency in office, this quality may therefore be justly regarded as an indispensable ingredient in its constitution; and in a great measure, as the citadel of the public justice and the public security.

The complete independence of the Courts of justice is peculiarly essential in a limited Constitution. By a limited Constitution, I understand one which contains certain specified exceptions to the Legislative authority; such, for instance, as that it shall pass no bills of attainder, no *ex post facto* laws, and the like. Limitations of this kind can be preserved in practice no other way than through the medium of the Courts of justice; whose duty it must be to declare all Acts contrary to the manifest tenor of the Constitution void. Without this, all the reservations of particular rights or privileges would amount to nothing.

Some perplexity respecting the rights of the Courts to pronounce Legislative acts void, because contrary to the Constitution, has arisen

1 The celebrated Montesquieu, speaking of them, says: "Of the three powers above mentioned, the judiciary is next to nothing." *Spirit of Laws*, Vol. I. page 186.—*Publius*.
2 *Idem*, page 181.—*Publius*.

from an imagination that the doctrine would imply a superiority of the Judiciary to the Legislative power. It is urged that the authority which can declare the acts of another void, must necessarily be superior to the one whose acts may be declared void. As this doctrine is of great importance in all the American Constitutions, a brief discussion of the ground on which it rests cannot be unacceptable.

There is no position which depends on clearer principles, than that every act of a delegated authority, contrary to the tenor of the commission under which it is exercised, is void. No Legislative act, therefore, contrary to the Constitution, can be valid. To deny this, would be to affirm, that the deputy is greater than his principal; that the servant is above his master; that the Representatives of the People are superior to the People themselves; that men acting by virtue of powers, may do not only what their powers do not authorize, but what they forbid.

If it be said that the Legislative body are themselves the constitutional judges of their own powers, and that the construction they put upon them is conclusive upon the other departments, it may be answered, that this cannot be the natural presumption, where it is not to be collected from any particular provisions in the Constitution. It is not otherwise to be supposed, that the Constitution could intend to enable the Representatives of the People to substitute their *will* to that of their constituents. It is far more rational to suppose, that the Courts were designed to be an intermediate body between the People and the Legislature, in order, among other things, to keep the latter within the limits assigned to their authority. The interpretation of the laws is the proper and peculiar province of the Courts. A Constitution is, in fact, and must be regarded by the Judges, as a fundamental law. It therefore belongs to them to ascertain its meaning, as well as the meaning of any particular Act proceeding from the Legislative body. If there should happen to be an irreconcilable variance between the two, that which has the superior obligation and validity ought, of course, to be preferred; or in other words, the Constitution ought to be preferred to the statute; the intention of the People to the intention of their agents.

Nor does this conclusion by any means suppose a superiority of the Judicial to the Legislative power. It only supposes that the power of the People is superior to both; and that where the will of the Legislature, declared in its statutes, stands in opposition to that of the People, declared in the Constitution, the Judges ought to be governed by the latter rather than the former. They ought to regulate their decisions by the fundamental laws, rather than by those which are not fundamental.

This exercise of judicial discretion, in determining between two contradictory laws, is exemplified in a familiar instance. It not uncommonly happens, that there are two statutes existing at one time, clashing in whole or in part with each other, and neither of them containing any repealing clause or expression. In such a case, it is the province of the Courts to liquidate and fix their meaning and operation; so far as they can, by any fair construction, be reconciled to each other, reason and law conspire to dictate that this should be done; where this is impracticable, it becomes a matter of necessity to give effect to one, in exclusion of the other. The rule which has obtained in the Courts for determining their relative validity is, that the last in order of time shall be preferred to the first. But this is a mere rule of construction, not derived from any positive law, but from the nature and reason of the thing. It is a rule not enjoined upon the Courts by Legislative provision, but adopted by themselves, as consonant to truth and propriety, for the direction of their conduct as interpreters of the law. They thought it reasonable, that between the interfering acts of an *equal* authority, that which was the last indication of its will should have the preference.

But in regard to the interfering acts of a superior and subordinate authority, of an original and derivative power, the nature and reason of the thing indicate the converse of that rule as proper to be followed. They teach us that the prior act of a superior ought to be preferred to the subsequent act of an inferior and subordinate authority; and that accordingly, whenever a particular statute contravenes the Constitution, it will be the duty of the Judicial tribunals to adhere to the latter and disregard the former.

It can be of no weight to say that the Courts, on the pretence of a repugnancy, may substitute their own pleasure to the constitutional intentions of the Legislature. This might as well happen in the case of two contradictory statutes; or it might as well happen in every adjudication upon any single statute. The Courts must declare the sense of the law; and if they should be disposed to exercise will instead of judgment, the consequence would equally be the substitution of their pleasure to that of the Legislative body. The observation, if it proved anything, would prove that there ought to be no Judges distinct from that body.

If then the Courts of justice are to be considered as the bulwarks of a limited Constitution, against Legislative encroachments, this consideration will afford a strong argument for the permanent tenure of Judicial offices, since nothing will contribute so much as this to that independent spirit in the Judges, which must be essential to the faithful performance of so arduous a duty.

This independence of the Judges is equally requisite to guard the Constitution and the rights of individuals, from the effects of those ill humors, which the arts of designing men, or the influence of particular conjunctures, sometimes disseminate among the People themselves, and which, though they speedily give place to better information, and more deliberate reflection, have a tendency, in the mean time, to occasion dangerous innovations in the Government, and serious oppressions of the minor party in the community. Though I trust the friends of the proposed Constitution will never concur with its enemies,3 in questioning that fundamental principle of republican Government, which admits the right of the People to alter or abolish the established Constitution, whenever they find it inconsistent with their happiness, yet it is not to be inferred from this principle, that the Representatives of the People, whenever a momentary inclination happens to lay hold of a majority of their constituents, incompatible with the provisions in the existing Constitution, would, on that account, be justifiable in a violation of those provisions; or that the Courts would be under a

3 Vide *Protest of the Minority of the Convention of Pennsylvania*, Martin's *Speech*, &c.—*Publius*.

greater obligation to connive at infractions in this shape, than when they had proceeded wholly from the cabals of the Representative body. Until the People have, by some solemn and authoritative act, annulled or changed the established form, it is binding upon themselves collectively, as well as individually; and no presumption, or even knowledge of their sentiments, can warrant their Representatives in a departure from it, prior to such an act. But it is easy to see, that it would require an uncommon portion of fortitude in the Judges to do their duty as faithful guardians of the Constitution, where Legislative invasions of it had been instigated by the major voice of the community.

But it is not with a view to infractions of the Constitution only, that the independence of the Judges may be an essential safeguard against the effects of occasional ill humors in the society. These sometimes extend no farther than to the injury of the private rights of particular classes of citizens, by unjust and partial laws. Here also the firmness of the Judicial magistracy is of vast importance in mitigating the severity, and confining the operation of such laws. It not only serves to moderate the immediate mischiefs of those which may have been passed, but it operates as a check upon the Legislative body in passing them; who, perceiving that obstacles to the success of iniquitous intention are to be expected from the scruples of the Courts, are in a manner compelled, by the very motives of the injustice they meditate, to qualify their attempts. This is a circumstance calculated to have more influence upon the character of our Governments, than but few may be aware of. The benefits of the integrity and moderation of the Judiciary have already been felt in more States than one; and though they may have displeased those whose sinister expectations they may have disappointed, they must have commanded the esteem and applause of all the virtuous and disinterested. Considerate men, of every description, ought to prize whatever will tend to beget or fortify that temper in the Courts; as no man can be sure that he may not be to-morrow the victim of a spirit of injustice, by which he may be a gainer to-day. And every man must now feel, that the inevitable tendency of such a spirit is to sap the foundations of public and private confidence, and to introduce in its stead universal distrust and distress.

That inflexible and uniform adherence to the rights of the Constitution, and of individuals, which we perceive to be indispensable in the Courts of justice, can certainly not be expected from Judges who hold their offices by a temporary commission. Periodical appointments, however regulated, or by whomsoever made, would, in some way or other, be fatal to their necessary independence. If the power of making them was committed either to the Executive or Legislature, there would be danger of an improper complaisance to the branch which possessed it; if to both, there would be an unwillingness to hazard the displeasure of either; if to the People, or to persons chosen by them for the special purpose, there would be too great a disposition to consult popularity, to justify a reliance that nothing would be consulted but the Constitution and the laws.

There is yet a further and a weightier reason for the permanency of the Judicial offices, which is deducible from the nature of the qualifications they require. It has been frequently remarked, with great propriety, that a voluminous code of laws is one of the inconveniences necessarily connected with the advantages of a free Government. To avoid an arbitrary discretion in the Courts, it is indispensable that they should be bound down by strict rules and precedents, which serve to define and point out their duty in every particular case that comes before them; and it will readily be conceived from the variety of controversies which grow out of the folly and wickedness of mankind, that the records of those precedents must unavoidably swell to a very considerable bulk, and must demand long and laborious study to acquire a competent knowledge of them. Hence it is, that there can be but few men in the society, who will have sufficient skill in the laws to qualify them for the stations of Judges. And making the proper deductions for the ordinary depravity of human nature, the number must be still smaller of those who unite the requisite integrity with the requisite knowledge. These considerations apprize us, that the Government can have no great option between fit characters; and that a temporary duration in office, which would naturally discourage such characters from quitting a lucrative line of practice to accept a seat on the Bench, would have a tendency to throw the administration of justice into hands less able, and less well qualified, to conduct it with utility and dignity. In the present circumstances of this country, and in those in which it is likely to be for a long time to come, the disadvantages on this score would be greater than they may at first sight appear; but it must be confessed, that they are far inferior to those which present themselves under the other aspects of the subject.

Upon the whole, there can be no room to doubt that the Convention acted wisely, in copying from the models of those Constitutions which have established *good behavior* as the tenure of their Judicial offices, in point of duration; and that so far from being blamable on this account, their plan would have been inexcusably defective, if it had wanted this important feature of good Government. The experience of Great Britain affords an illustrious comment on the excellence of the institution.

PUBLIUS.

MARTIN LUTHER KING, JR.: LETTER FROM BIRMINGHAM JAIL

Martin Luther King, Jr.
Birmingham City Jail
April 16, 1963

My dear Fellow Clergymen,

While confined here in the Birmingham City Jail, I came across your recent statement calling our present activities "unwise and untimely." Seldom, if ever, do I pause to answer criticism of my work and ideas. If I sought to answer all the criticisms that cross my desk, my secretaries would be engaged in little else in the course of the day and I would have no time for constructive work. But since I feel that you are men of genuine goodwill and your criticisms are sincerely set forth, I would like to answer your statement in what I hope will be patient and reasonable terms.

I think I should give the reason for my being in Birmingham, since you have been influenced by the argument of "outsiders coming in." I have the honor of serving as president of the Southern Christian Leadership Conference, an organization operating in every Southern state with headquarters in Atlanta, Georgia. We have some eighty-five affiliate organizations all across the South—one being the Alabama Christian Movement for Human Rights. Whenever necessary and possible we share staff, educational, and financial resources with our affiliates. Several months ago our local affiliate here in Birmingham invited us to be on call to engage in a nonviolent direct action program if such were deemed necessary. We readily consented and when the hour came we lived up to our promises. So I am here, along with several members of my staff, because we were invited here. I am here because I have basic organizational ties here. Beyond this, I am in Birmingham because injustice is here. Just as the eighth century prophets left their little villages and carried their "thus saith the Lord" far beyond the boundaries of their home town, and just as the Apostle Paul left his little village of Tarsus and carried the gospel of Jesus Christ to practically every hamlet and city of the Graeco-Roman world, I too am compelled to carry the gospel of freedom beyond my particular home town. Like Paul, I must constantly respond to the Macedonian call for aid.

Moreover, I am cognizant of the interrelatedness of all communities and states. I cannot sit idly by in Atlanta and not be concerned about what happens in Birmingham. Injustice anywhere is a threat to justice everywhere. We are caught in an inescapable network of mutuality tied in a single garment of destiny. Whatever affects one directly affects all indirectly. Never again can we afford to live with the narrow, provincial "outside agitator" idea. Anyone who lives inside the United States can never be considered an outsider anywhere in this country.

You deplore the demonstrations that are presently taking place in Birmingham. But I am sorry that your statement did not express a similar concern for the conditions that brought the demonstrations into being. I am sure that each of you would want to go beyond the superficial social analyst who looks merely at effects, and does not grapple with underlying causes. I would not hesitate to say that it is unfortunate that so-called demonstrations are taking place in Birmingham at this time, but I would say in more emphatic terms that it is even more unfortunate that the white power structure of this city left the Negro community with no other alternative.

In any nonviolent campaign there are four basic steps: (1) Collection of the facts to determine whether injustices are alive; (2) Negotiation; (3) Self-purification; and (4) Direct action. We have gone through all of these steps in Birmingham. There can be no gainsaying of the fact that racial injustice engulfs this community. Birmingham is probably the most thoroughly segregated city in the United States. Its ugly record of police brutality is known in every section of this country. Its unjust treatment of Negroes in the courts is a notorious reality. There have been more unsolved bombings of Negro homes and churches in Birmingham than any city in this nation. These are the hard, brutal, and unbelievable facts. On the basis of these conditions Negro leaders sought to negotiate with the city fathers. But the political leaders consistently refused to engage in good faith negotiation.

Then came the opportunity last September to talk with some of the leaders of the economic community. In these negotiating sessions certain promises were made by the merchants—such as the promise to remove the humiliating racial signs from the stores. On the basis of these promises Rev. Shuttlesworth and the leaders of the Alabama Christian Movement for Human Rights agreed to call a moratorium on any type of demonstrations. As the weeks and months unfolded we realized that we were the victims of a broken promise. The signs remained. As in so many experiences of the past we were confronted with blasted hopes, and the dark shadow of a deep disappointment settled upon us. So we had no alternative except that of preparing for direct action, whereby we would present our very bodies as a means of laying our case before the conscience of the local and national community. We were not unmindful of the difficulties involved. So we decided to go through a process of self-purification. We started having workshops on nonviolence and repeatedly asked ourselves the questions, "Are you able to accept blows without retaliating?" "Are you able to endure the ordeals of jail?"

We decided to set our direct-action program around the Easter season, realizing that with the exception of Christmas, this was the largest shopping period of the year. Knowing that a strong economic withdrawal program would be the by-product of direct action, we felt that this was the best time to bring pressure on the merchants for the needed changes. Then it occurred to us that the March election was ahead, and so we speedily decided to postpone action until after election day. When we discovered that Mr. Connor was in the run-off, we decided again to postpone action so that the demonstrations could not be used to cloud the issues. At this time we agreed to begin our nonviolent witness the day after the run-off.

This reveals that we did not move irresponsibly into direct action. We too wanted to see Mr. Connor defeated; so we went through postponement after postponement to aid in this community need. After this we felt that direct action could be delayed no longer.

You may well ask, Why direct action? Why sit-ins, marches, etc.? Isn't negotiation a better path?" You are exactly right in your call for negotiation. Indeed, this is the purpose of direct action. Nonviolent direct action seeks to create such a crisis and establish such creative tension that a community that has constantly refused to negotiate is forced to confront the issue. It seeks so to dramatize the issue that it can no longer be ignored. I just referred to the creation of tension as a part of the work of the nonviolent resister. This may sound rather shocking. But I must confess that I am not afraid of the word tension. I have earnestly worked and preached against violent tension, but there is a type of constructive nonviolent tension that is necessary for growth. Just as Socrates felt that it was necessary to create a tension in the mind so that individuals could rise from the bondage of myths and half-truths to the unfettered realm of creative analysis and objective appraisal, we must see the need of having nonviolent gadflies to create the kind of tension in society that will help men rise from the dark depths of prejudice and racism to the majestic heights of understanding and brotherhood. So the purpose of the direct action is to create a situation so crisis-packed that it will inevitably open the door to negotiation. We, therefore, concur with you in your call for negotiation. Too long has our beloved Southland been bogged down in the tragic attempt to live in monologue rather than dialogue.

One of the basic points in your statement is that our acts are untimely. Some have asked, "Why didn't you give the new administration time to act?" The only answer that I can give to this inquiry is that the new administration must be prodded about as much as the outgoing one before it acts. We will be sadly mistaken if we feel that the election of Mr. Boutwell will bring the millennium to Birmingham. While Mr. Boutwell is much more articulate and gentle than Mr. Connor, they are both segregationists dedicated to the task of maintaining the status quo. The hope I see in Mr. Boutwell is that he will be reasonable enough to see the futility of massive resistance to desegregation. But he will not see this without pressure from the devotees of civil rights. My friends, I must say to you that we have not made a single gain in civil rights without determined legal and nonviolent pressure. History is the long and tragic story of the fact that privileged groups seldom give up their privileges voluntarily. Individuals may see the moral light and voluntarily give up their unjust posture; but as Reinhold Niebuhr has reminded us, groups are more immoral than individuals.

We know through painful experience that freedom is never voluntarily given by the oppressor; it must be demanded by the oppressed. Frankly I have never yet engaged in a direct action movement that was "well timed," according to the timetable of those who have not suffered unduly from the disease of segregation. For years now I have heard the word "Wait!" It rings in the ear of every Negro with a piercing familiarity. This "wait" has almost always meant "never." It has been a tranquilizing thalidomide, relieving the emotional stress for a moment, only to give birth to an ill-formed infant of frustration. We must come to see with the distinguished jurist of yesterday that "justice too long delayed is justice denied." We have waited for more than three hundred and forty years for our constitutional and God-given rights. The nations of Asia and Africa are moving with jet-like speed toward the goal of political independence, and we still creep at horse and buggy pace toward the gaining of a cup of coffee at a lunch counter.

I guess it is easy for those who have never felt the stinging darts of segregation to say wait. But when you have seen vicious mobs lynch your mothers and fathers at will and drown your sisters and brothers at whim; when you have seen hate filled policemen curse, kick, brutalize, and even kill your black brothers and sisters with impunity;

when you see the vast majority of your twenty million Negro brothers smothering in an air-tight cage of poverty in the midst of an affluent society; when you suddenly find your tongue twisted and your speech stammering as you seek to explain to your six-year-old daughter why she can't go to the public amusement park that has just been advertised on television, and see tears welling up in her little eyes when she is told that Funtown is closed to colored children, and see the depressing clouds of inferiority begin to form in her little mental sky, and see her begin to distort her little personality by unconsciously developing a bitterness toward white people; when you have to concoct an answer for a five-year-old son asking in agonizing pathos: "Daddy, why do white people treat colored people so mean?"; when you take a cross-country drive and find it necessary to sleep night after night in the uncomfortable corners of your automobile because no motel will accept you; when you are humiliated day in and day out by nagging signs reading "white" men and "colored"; when your first name becomes "nigger" and your middle name becomes "boy" (however old you are) and your last name becomes "John," and when your wife and mother are never given the respected title "Mrs."; when you are harried by day and haunted by night by the fact that you are a Negro, living constantly at tip-toe stance never quite knowing what to expect next, and plagued with inner fears and outer resentments; when you are forever fighting a degenerating sense of "nobodiness"—then you will understand why we find it difficult to wait. There comes a time when the cup of endurance runs over, and men are no longer willing to be plunged into an abyss of injustice where they experience the bleakness of corroding despair. I hope, sirs, you can understand our legitimate and unavoidable impatience.

You express a great deal of anxiety over our willingness to break laws. This is certainly a legitimate concern. Since we so diligently urge people to obey the Supreme Court's decision of 1954 outlawing segregation in the public schools, it is rather strange and paradoxical to find us consciously breaking laws. One may well ask: "How can you advocate breaking some laws and obeying others?" The answer is found in the fact that there are two types of laws: There are just laws and there are unjust laws. I would be the first to advocate obeying just laws. One has not only a legal but moral responsibility to obey just laws. Conversely, one has a moral responsibility to disobey unjust laws. I would agree with Saint Augustine that "An unjust law is no law at all."

Now what is the difference between the two? How does one determine when a law is just or unjust? A just law is a man-made code that squares with the moral law or the law of God. An unjust law is a code that is out of harmony with the moral law. To put it in the terms of Saint Thomas Aquinas, an unjust law is a human law that is not rooted in eternal and natural law. Any law that uplifts human personality is just. Any law that degrades human personality is unjust. All segregation statutes are unjust because segregation distorts the soul and damages the personality. It gives the segregator a false sense of superiority and the segregated a false sense of inferiority. To use the words of Martin Buber, the great Jewish philosopher, segregation substitutes an "I-it" relationship for an "I-thou" relationship, and ends up relegating persons to the status of things. So segregation is not only politically, economically, and sociologically unsound, but it is morally wrong and sinful. Paul Tillich has said that sin is separation. Isn't segregation an existential expression of man's tragic separation, an expression of his awful estrangement, his terrible sinfulness? So I can urge men to obey the1954 decision of the Supreme Court because it is morally right, and I can urge them to disobey segregation ordinances because they are morally wrong.

Let us turn to a more concrete example of just and unjust laws. An unjust law is a code that a majority inflicts on a minority that is not binding on itself. This is *difference* made legal. On the other hand a just law is a code that a majority compels a minority to follow that it is willing to follow itself. This is *sameness* made legal.

Let me give another explanation. An unjust law is a code inflicted upon a minority which that minority had no part in enacting or creating because they did not have the unhampered right to vote. Who can say that the legislature of Alabama which set up the segregation laws was democratically elected? Throughout the state of Alabama all types of conniving methods are used to prevent Negroes from becoming registered voters and there are some counties without a single Negro registered to vote despite the fact that the Negro constitutes a majority of the population. Can any law set up in such a state be considered democratically structured?

These are just a few examples of unjust and just laws. There are some instances when a law is just on its face but unjust in its application. For instance, I was arrested Friday on a charge of parading without a permit. Now there is nothing wrong with an ordinance which requires a permit for a parade, but when the ordinance is used to preserve segregation and to deny citizens the First Amendment privilege of peaceful assembly and peaceful protest, then it becomes unjust.

I hope you can see the distinction I am trying to point out. In no sense do I advocate evading or defying the law as the rabid segregationist would do. This would lead to anarchy. One who breaks an unjust law must do it *openly, lovingly* (not hatefully as the white mothers did in New Orleans when they were seen on television screaming "nigger, nigger, nigger") and with a willingness to accept the penalty. I submit that an individual who breaks a law that conscience tells him is unjust, and willingly accepts the penalty by staying in jail to arouse the conscience of the community over its injustice, is in reality expressing the very highest respect for law.

Of course there is nothing new about this kind of civil disobedience. It was seen sublimely in the refusal of Shadrach, Meshach, and Abednego to obey the laws of Nebuchadnezzar because a higher moral law was involved. It was practiced superbly by the early Christians who were willing to face hungry lions and the excruciating pain of chopping blocks, before submitting to certain unjust laws of the Roman Empire. To a degree academic freedom is a reality today because Socrates practiced civil disobedience.

We can never forget that everything Hitler did in Germany was "legal" and everything the Hungarian freedom fighters did in Hungary was "illegal." It was "illegal" to aid and comfort a Jew in Hitler's Germany. But I am sure that, if I had lived in Germany during that time, I would have aided and comforted my Jewish brothers even though it was illegal. If I lived in a communist country today where certain principles dear to the Christian faith are suppressed, I believe I would openly advocate disobeying these anti-religious laws.

I must make two honest confessions to you, my Christian and Jewish brothers. First, I must confess that over the last few years I have been gravely disappointed with the white moderate. I have almost reached the regrettable conclusion that the Negroes' great stumbling block in the stride toward freedom is not the White Citizen's "Counciler" or the Ku Klux Klanner, but the white moderate who is more devoted to "order" than to justice; who prefers a negative peace which is the absence of tension to a positive peace which is the presence of justice; who constantly says "I agree with you in the goal you seek, but I can't agree with your methods of direct action"; who paternalistically feels that he can set the timetable for another man's freedom; who lives by the myth of time and who constantly advises the Negro to wait until a "more convenient season." Shallow understanding from people of good will is more frustrating than absolute misunderstanding from people of ill will. Lukewarm acceptance is much more bewildering than outright rejection.

I had hoped that the white moderate would understand that law and order exist for the purpose of establishing justice, and that when they fail to do this they become dangerously structured dams that block the flow of social progress. I had hoped that the white moderate would understand that the present tension in the South is merely a necessary phase of the transition from an obnoxious negative peace, where the Negro passively accepted his unjust plight, to a substance-filled positive peace, where all men will respect the dignity and worth of human personality. Actually, we who engage in nonviolent direct action are not the creators of tension. We merely bring to the surface the hidden tension that is already alive. We bring it out in the open where it can be seen and dealt with. Like a boil that can never be cured as long as it is covered up but must be opened with all its pus-flowing ugliness to the natural medicines of air and light, injustice must likewise be exposed, with all of the tension its exposing creates, to the light of human conscience and the air of national opinion before it can be cured.

In your statement you asserted that our actions, even though peaceful, must be condemned because they precipitate violence. But can this assertion be logically made? Isn't this like condemning the robbed man because his possession of money precipitated the evil act of robbery? Isn't this like condemning Socrates because his unswerving commitment to truth and his philosophical delvings precipitated the misguided popular mind to make him drink the hemlock? Isn't this like condemning Jesus because His unique God consciousness and never-ceasing devotion to His will precipitated the evil act of crucifixion? We must come to see, as federal courts have consistently affirmed, that it is immoral to urge an individual to withdraw his efforts to gain his basic constitutional rights because the quest precipitates violence. Society must protect the robbed and punish the robber.

I had also hoped that the white moderate would reject the myth of time. I received a letter this morning from a white brother in Texas which said: "All Christians know that the colored people will receive equal rights eventually, but is it possible that you are in too great of a religious hurry? It has taken Christianity almost 2,000 years to accomplish what it has. The teachings of Christ take time to come to earth." All that is said here grows out of a tragic misconception of time. It is the strangely irrational notion that there is something in the very flow of time that will inevitably cure all ills. Actually time is neutral. It can be used either destructively or constructively. I am coming to feel that the people of ill will have used time much more effectively than the people of good will. We will have to repent in this generation not merely for the vitriolic words and actions of the bad people, but for the appalling silence of the good people. We must come to see that human progress never rolls in on wheels of inevitability. It comes through the tireless efforts and persistent work of men willing to be co-workers with God, and without this hard work time itself becomes an ally of the forces of social stagnation.

We must use time creatively, and forever realize that the time is always ripe to do right. Now is the time to make real the promise of democracy, and transform our pending national elegy into a creative psalm of brotherhood. Now is the time to lift our national policy from the quicksand of racial injustice to the solid rock of human dignity.

You spoke of our activity in Birmingham as extreme. At first I was rather disappointed that fellow clergymen would see my nonviolent efforts as those of the extremist. I started thinking about the fact that I stand in the middle of two opposing forces in the Negro community. One is a force of complacency made up of Negroes who, as a result of long years of oppression, have been so completely drained of self-respect and a sense of "somebodiness" that they have adjusted to segregation, and of a few Negroes in the middle class who, because of a degree of academic and economic security, and because at points they profit by segregation, have unconsciously become insensitive to the problems of the masses. The other force is one of bitterness and hatred and comes perilously close to advocating violence. It is expressed in the various black nationalist groups that are springing up over the nation, the largest and best known being Elijah Muhammad's Muslim movement. This movement is nourished by the contemporary frustration over the continued existence of racial discrimination. It is made up of people who have lost faith in America, who have absolutely repudiated Christianity, and who have concluded that the white man is an incurable "devil." I have tried to stand between these two forces saying that we need not follow the "do-nothingism" of the complacent or the hatred and despair of the black nationalist. There is the more excellent way of love and nonviolent protest. I'm grateful to God that, through the Negro church, the dimension of nonviolence entered our struggle. If this philosophy had not emerged I am convinced that by now many streets of the South would be flowing with floods of blood. And I am further convinced that if our white brothers dismiss us as "rabble rousers" and "outside agitators"—those of us who are working through the channels of nonviolent direct action—and refuse to support our nonviolent efforts, millions of Negroes, out of frustration and despair, will seek solace and security in black-nationalist ideologies, a development that will lead inevitably to a frightening racial nightmare.

Oppressed people cannot remain oppressed forever. The urge for freedom will eventually come. This is what has happened to the American Negro. Something within has reminded him of his birthright of freedom; something without has reminded him that he can gain it. Consciously and unconsciously, he has been swept in by what the Germans call the *Zeitgeist*, and with his black brothers of Africa, and his brown and yellow brothers of Asia, South America, and the Caribbean, he is moving with a sense of cosmic urgency toward the promised land of racial justice. Recognizing this vital urge that has engulfed the Negro community, one should readily understand public demonstrations. The Negro has many pent-up resentments and latent frustrations. He has to get them out. So let him march sometime; let him have his prayer pilgrimages to the city hall; understand why he must have sit-ins and freedom rides. If his repressed emotions do not come out in these nonviolent ways, they will come out in ominous expressions of violence. This is not a threat; it is a fact of history. So I have not said to my people, "Get rid of your discontent." But I have tried to say that this normal and healthy discontent can be channeled through the creative outlet of nonviolent direct action. Now this approach is being dismissed as extremist. I must admit that I was initially disappointed in being so categorized.

But as I continued to think about the matter I gradually gained a bit of satisfaction from being considered an extremist. Was not Jesus an extremist in love? "Love your enemies, bless them that curse you, pray for them that despitefully use you." Was not Amos an extremist for justice—"Let justice roll down like waters and righteousness like a mighty stream." Was not Paul an extremist for the gospel of Jesus Christ—"I bear in my body the marks of the Lord Jesus." Was not Martin Luther an extremist—"Here I stand; I can do none other so help me God." Was not John Bunyan an extremist—"I will stay in jail to the end of my days before I make a butchery of my conscience." Was not Abraham Lincoln an extremist—"This nation cannot survive half slave and half free." Was not Thomas Jefferson an extremist—"We hold these truths to be self-evident, that all men are created equal." So the question is not whether we will be extremist but what kind of extremist will we be. Will we be extremists for hate or will we be extremists for love? Will we be extremists for the preservation of injustice—or will we be extremists for the cause of justice? In that dramatic scene on Calvary's hill three men were crucified. We must never forget that all three were crucified for the same crime—the crime of extremism. Two were extremists for immorality, and thus fell below their environment. The other, Jesus Christ, was an extremist for love, truth, and goodness, and thereby rose above His environment. So, after all, maybe the South, the nation, and the world are in dire need of creative extremists.

I had hoped that the white moderate would see this. Maybe I was too optimistic. Maybe I expected too much. I guess I should have realized that few members of a race that has oppressed another race can understand or appreciate the deep groans and passionate yearnings of those that have been oppressed, and still fewer have the vision to see that injustice must be rooted out by strong, persistent, and determined action. I am thankful, however, that some of our white brothers have grasped the meaning of this social revolution and committed themselves to it. They are still all too small in quantity, but they are big in quality. Some like Ralph McGill, Lillian Smith, Harry Golden, and James Dabbs have written about our struggle in eloquent, prophetic, and understanding terms. Others have marched with us down nameless streets of the South. They have languished in filthy, roach-infested jails, suffering the abuse and brutality of angry policemen who see them as "dirty nigger lovers." They, unlike so many of their moderate brothers and sisters, have recognized the urgency of the moment and sensed the need for powerful "action" antidotes to combat the disease of segregation.

Let me rush on to mention my other disappointment. I have been so greatly disappointed with the white Church and its leadership. Of course there are some notable exceptions. I am not unmindful of the fact that each of you has taken some significant stands on this issue. I commend you, Rev. Stallings, for your Christian stand on this past Sunday, in welcoming Negroes to your worship service on a non-segregated basis. I commend the Catholic leaders of this state for integrating Spring Hill College several years ago.

But despite these notable exceptions I must honestly reiterate that I have been disappointed with the Church. I do not say that as one of those negative critics who can always find something wrong with the Church. I say it as a minister of the gospel, who loves the Church; who was nurtured in its bosom; who has been sustained by its spiritual blessings and who will remain true to it as long as the cord of life shall lengthen.

I had the strange feeling when I was suddenly catapulted into the leadership of the bus protest in Montgomery several years ago that we would have the support of the white Church. I felt that the white ministers, priests, and rabbis of the South would be some of our strongest allies. Instead, some have been outright opponents, refusing to understand the freedom movement and misrepresenting its leaders; all too many others have been more cautious than courageous and have remained silent behind the anesthetizing security of the stained glass windows.

In spite of my shattered dreams of the past, I came to Birmingham with the hope that the white religious leadership of this community would see the justice of our cause and with deep moral concern, serve as the channel through which our just grievances could get to the power structure. I had hoped that each of you would understand. But again I have been disappointed.

I have heard numerous religious leaders of the South call upon their worshippers to comply with a desegregation decision because it is the law, but I have longed to hear white ministers say follow this decree because integration is morally right and the Negro is your brother. In the midst of blatant injustices inflicted upon the Negro, I have watched white churches stand on the sideline and merely mouth pious irrelevancies and sanctimonious trivialities. In the midst of a mighty struggle to rid our nation of racial and economic injustice, I have heard so many ministers say, "Those are social issues with which the gospel has no real concern," and I have watched so many churches commit themselves to a completely other-worldly religion which made a strange distinction between body and soul, the sacred and the secular.

So here we are moving toward the exit of the twentieth century with a religious community largely adjusted to the status quo, standing as a tail-light behind other community agencies rather than a headlight leading men to higher levels of justice.

I have travelled the length and breadth of Alabama, Mississippi and all the other southern states. On sweltering summer days and crisp autumn mornings I have looked at her beautiful churches with their spires pointing heavenward. I have beheld the impressive outlay of her massive religious education buildings. Over and over again I have found myself asking: "Who worships here? Who is their God? Where were their voices when the lips of Governor Barnett dripped with words of interposition and nullification? Where were they when Governor Wallace gave the clarion call for defiance and hatred? Where were their voices of support when tired, bruised, and weary Negro men and women decided to rise from the dark dungeons of complacency to the bright hills of creative protest?"

Yes, these questions are still in my mind. In deep disappointment, I have wept over the laxity of the church. But be assured that my tears have been tears of love. There can be no deep disappointment where there is not deep love. Yes, I love the Church; I love her sacred walls. How could I do otherwise? I am in the rather unique position of being the son, the grandson, and the great-grandson of preachers. Yes, I see the Church as the body of Christ. But, oh! How we have blemished and scarred that body through social neglect and fear of being nonconformist.

There was a time when the Church was very powerful. It was during that period when the early Christians rejoiced when they were deemed worthy to suffer for what they believed. In those days the Church was not merely a thermometer that recorded the ideas and principles of popular opinion; it was a thermostat that transformed the mores of society. Wherever the early Christians entered a town the power structure got disturbed and immediately sought to convict them for being "disturbers of the peace" and "outside agitators." But they went on with the conviction that they were "a colony of heaven" and had to obey God rather than man. They were small in number but big in commitment. They were too God-intoxicated to be "astronomically intimidated." They brought an end to such ancient evils as infanticide and gladiatorial contest.

Things are different now. The contemporary Church is so often a weak, ineffectual voice with an uncertain sound. It is so often the arch-supporter of the status quo. Far from being disturbed by the presence of the Church, the power structure of the average community is consoled by the Church's silent and often vocal sanction of things as they are.

But the judgment of God is upon the Church as never before. If the Church of today does not recapture the sacrificial spirit of the early Church, it will lose its authentic ring, forfeit the loyalty of millions, and be dismissed as an irrelevant social club with no meaning for the twentieth century. I am meeting young people every day whose disappointment with the Church has risen to outright disgust.

Maybe again I have been too optimistic. Is organized religion too inextricably bound to the status quo to save our nation and the world? Maybe I must turn my faith to the inner spiritual Church, the church within the Church, as the true ecclesia and the hope of the world. But again I am thankful to God that some noble souls from the ranks of organized religion have broken loose from the paralyzing chains of conformity and joined us as active partners in the struggle for freedom. They have left their secure congregations and walked the streets of Albany, Georgia, with us. They have gone through the highways of the South on torturous rides for freedom. Yes, they have gone to jail with us. Some have been kicked out of their churches and lost the support of their bishops and fellow ministers. But they have gone with the faith that right defeated is stronger than evil triumphant. These men have been the leaven in the lump of the race. Their witness has been the spiritual salt that has preserved the true meaning of the Gospel in these troubled times. They have carved a tunnel of hope through the dark mountain of disappointment.

I hope the Church as a whole will meet the challenge of this decisive hour. But even if the Church does not come to the aid of justice, I have no despair about the future. I have no fear about the outcome of our struggle in Birmingham, even if our motives are presently misunderstood. We will reach the goal of freedom in Birmingham and all over the nation, because the goal of America is freedom. Abused and scorned though we may be, our destiny is tied up with the destiny of America. Before the pilgrims landed at Plymouth, we were here. Before the pen of Jefferson etched across the pages of history the majestic words of the Declaration of Independence, we were here. For more than two centuries our foreparents labored in this country without wages; they made cotton "king"; and they built the homes of their masters in the midst of brutal injustice and shameful humiliation—and yet out of a bottomless vitality they continued to thrive and develop. If the inexpressible cruelties of slavery could not stop us, the opposition we now face will surely fail. We will win our freedom because the sacred heritage of our nation and the eternal will of God are embodied in our echoing demands.

I must close now. But before closing I am impelled to mention one other point in your statement that troubled me profoundly. You warmly commend the Birmingham police force for keeping "order" and "preventing violence." I don't believe you would have so warmly commended the police force if you had seen its angry violent dogs literally biting six unarmed, nonviolent Negroes. I don't believe you would so quickly commend the policemen if you would observe their ugly and inhuman treatment of Negroes here in the city jail; if you would watch them push and curse old Negro women and young Negro girls; if you would see them slap and kick old Negro men and young Negro boys; if you will observe them, as they did on two occasions, refuse to give us food because we wanted to sing our grace together. I'm sorry that I can't join you in your praise for the police department.

It is true that they have been rather disciplined in their public handling of the demonstrators. In this sense they have been rather publicly "nonviolent." But for what purpose? To preserve the evil system of segregation. Over the last few years I have consistently preached that nonviolence demands the means we use must be as pure as the ends we seek. So I have tried to make it clear that it is wrong to use immoral means to attain moral ends. But now I must affirm that it is just as wrong or even more so to use moral means to preserve immoral ends. Maybe Mr. Connor and his policemen have been rather publicly nonviolent, as Chief Pritchett was in Albany, Georgia, but they have used the moral means of nonviolence to maintain the immoral end of flagrant injustice. T. S. Eliot has said that there is no greater treason than to do the right deed for the wrong reason.

I wish you had commended the Negro sit-inners and demonstrators of Birmingham for their sublime courage, their willingness to suffer, and their amazing discipline in the midst of the most inhuman provocation. One day the South will recognize its real heroes. They will be the James Merediths, courageously and with a majestic sense of purpose, facing jeering and hostile mobs and the agonizing loneliness that characterizes the life of the pioneer. They will be old, oppressed, battered Negro women, symbolized in a seventy-two year old woman of Montgomery, Alabama, who rose up with a sense of dignity and with her people decided not to ride the segregated buses, and responded to one who inquired about her tiredness with ungrammatical profundity: "My feets is tired, but my soul is rested." They will be the young high school and college students, young ministers of the gospel and a host of their elders courageously and nonviolently sitting-in at lunch counters and willingly going to jail for conscience sake. One day the South will know that when these disinherited children of God sat down at lunch counters they were in reality standing up for the best in the American dream and the most sacred values in our Judaeo-Christian heritage, and thus carrying our whole nation back to great wells of democracy which were dug deep by the founding fathers in the formulation of the Constitution and the Declaration of Independence.

Never before have I written a letter this long (or should I say a book?). I'm afraid it is much too long to take your precious time. I can assure you that it would have been much shorter if I had been writing from a comfortable desk, but what else is there to do when you are alone for days in the dull monotony of a narrow jail cell other than write long letters, think strange thoughts, and pray long prayers?

If I have said anything in this letter that is an overstatement of the truth and is indicative of an unreasonable impatience, I beg you to forgive me. If I have said anything in this letter that is an understatement of the truth and is indicative of my having a patience that makes me patient with anything less than brotherhood, I beg God to forgive me.

I hope this letter finds you strong in the faith. I also hope that circumstances will soon make it possible for me to meet each of you, not as an integrationist or a civil rights leader, but as a fellow clergyman and a Christian brother. Let us all hope that the dark clouds of racial prejudice will soon pass away and the deep fog of misunderstanding will be lifted from our fear-drenched communities and in some not too distant tomorrow the radiant stars of love and brotherhood will shine over our great nation with all their scintillating beauty.

Yours for the cause of
Peace and Brotherhood,

Martin Luther King, Jr.

CPSIA information can be obtained
at www.ICGtesting.com
Printed in the USA
LVOW02s0005090116
469710LV00005B/7/P

9 781634 87408